How to Say It®

TO YOUR CHILD WHEN BAD THINGS HAPPEN

How to Say It®

TO YOUR CHILD WHEN BAD THINGS HAPPEN

Good Answers to
Tough Questions

DR. PAUL COLEMAN

Prentice Hall Press

A member of Penguin Putnam Inc.
375 Hudson Street
New York, New York, 10014

http://www.penguinputnam.com

First Prentice Hall Press edition: October 2002

Library of Congress Cataloging-in-Publication Data

Coleman, Paul W.
    How to say it to your child when bad things happen / Paul Coleman.—1st Prentice Hall Press ed.
        p.   cm.
    Includes bibliographical references (p.) and index.
    ISBN 0-7352-0325-3
    1. Interpersonal communication in children.   2. Communication in the family.   3. Parent and child.
    4. Children and adults.   I. Title.

BF723.C57 C585   2002
155.4'136—dc21

                                                                            2002074973

Printed in the United States of America

10   9   8   7   6   5   4   3   2   1

*To my loving wife, Jody,
and our children,
Luke, Anna, and Julia.*

Contents

PART THREE

The Work Phase of Trauma, Tragedy, or Terror

PART FOUR

The Well-Being Phase of Trauma, Tragedy, or Terror

Acknowledgments

I owe a large debt of gratitude to my literary agents, Mike and Patricia Snell. They never falter in their excitement, their professionalism, their generosity, or their friendliness.

I'm delighted to once again work with senior editor Tom Power at Prentice-Hall. This book would not have been written without his enthusiasm and vision.

Gina Walter deserves kudos for her tireless efforts at publicity on my last book. I wish her the best in her new profession. She will be a terrific teacher. Thanks also to Sharon L. Gonzalez, Francesca Drago, Yvette Romero and Lisa Giassa at Prentice Hall for their professionalism and talent.

Thu Nguyen was immensely helpful and most gracious with his time by revisiting the events of April 19, 1995, and explaining how the Oklahoma City bombing affected him and his family.

I also wish to thank my brother, John Coleman, assistant principal at J.F.K. Middle School in Enfield, Connecticut, for his help with getting comments from students who were quoted in this book. So many students contributed their thoughts and insights and all should be congratulated for their effort. In particular, I wish to thank the following students whose comments I chose to include in this book: Alicia Argenta, Amy Bourgoin, Lea Collins, Steve Davis, Nick Gallo, Antwan Jones, Courtney Kozlowski, Chelsea Lessard, Rachel Lindsey, Amber McEachern, Kristine Michaud, Jeff Nicoll, Nicole Ray, Jesse Ready, Shivani Shah, and Adam Varnet.

Thanks to Paul Tobin, principal, and Raymond Meunier, English department chair at Haldane Junior and Senior High School in Cold Spring, New York. They helped gather thoughts from their students on the 9/11 tragedy. Special thanks to Haldane students Katie Caliendo, Krista Fleming, and Isle Lansdale for their contributions.

Special thanks to Anna and Julia Coleman and Nicole Busch for their questions and insights.

I am grateful to Tom Lawrence for providing a quote from his daughter, Victoria; and to Joe Salamone for the quote from his son, Kyle.

Reflections of the 9/11 Tragedy

I was standing in a valley clearing surrounded by a dense forest. Suddenly, a river of faces diverged in front of me. Some were distantly familiar, some were not, for they were the ones I passed each day on the street but never cared to acknowledge. There they all were, and there I was, and suddenly a great herd of hoofed beasts erupted from the hills that surrounded me. They hurled me about with their great hooves and haunches, not one of them even caring to notice who was beneath them as they forded the river. It was all so amazing. But I never came to understand it and I probably never will.

—Ilse L., age 13

To those who died, I never knew life without you could be so rough . . . here is a long kiss good night.

—Antwan J., age 14

Part One

Guidelines for Parents and Other Caretakers

Children in the Middle East have suffered through terrorism and periodic wars for years. The last time that American children were subjected to intense fears of disaster or annihilation was in 1962 during the Cold War and the Cuban Missile Crisis. Schools showed films that explained how children should block their eyes or run to a nearby basement if a huge flash of light (a nuclear blast) appeared in the sky. Air raid shelters were commonplace. Seven-year-old kids practiced drills where they had to crouch beneath their desks in school. The Soviet leader promised he would "bury" America. A nuclear holocaust was as close to a certainty as it had ever been.

Fast-forward many decades.

Fears of a nuclear holocaust have reemerged, along with fears of devastating terrorist strikes and random, shocking violence such as school shootings. The freedom and relative safety we took for granted has been jostled. And people must once again find ways to live normal lives and yet somehow accommodate to new worries and concerns.

Adults must also talk to the children so they, too, can cope well and live their lives as children should live them.

Part One of this book will give general guidelines on talking to kids when bad things happen and the world is a scary place, emphasizing the all-important SAFE approach to dialogue. More specific, fine-tuned advice will be offered in the remainder of the book.

When Bad Things Happen and the World Becomes a Scary Place

Daddy's building on fire!

—Jason B., age 4, calling to his mother while watching the first
scenes of the World Trade Center disaster on television

Is our school safe?

—Bobby M., age 7, overheard talking to a classmate after
hearing news about the Columbine school shooting

Even though no one in my family died, I felt like I was going to cry.

—Katie C., age 16, referring to the 9/11 tragedy

The remedy for fear is trust.

But look at what.has happened in the world in recent years: the World Trade Center; the Pentagon; Oklahoma City; Columbine, and a string of other school shootings; physical and sexual abuse; AIDS; McVeigh; bin Laden; anthrax; terrorism; suicide bombings in the Mid-East; plane crashes; the Gulf War; Afghanistan, and the prospect of more wars.

Many of those events and infamous people are seared into the photo album of our collective memory, and our children's memories. They are powerful, graphic snapshots taken during the time of our children's youth, snapshots that *their* kids—our grandkids—will stare at in the history books yet to be written.

Then there are the natural disasters that have increased dramatically over the past decade: floods, hurricanes, tornadoes, devastating blizzards—even a flurry of shark attacks. Whether they are experienced firsthand, viewed on the evening news, or spoken about in the school lunchroom, thousands of children are hurt or frightened each year.

The fact cannot be ignored that almost overnight the world has become a scarier place. Our children are counting on us to protect them, reassure them, never give them reason to doubt our devotion to them, and in most cases, to explain to them what it all means and how their lives will be affected.

The remedy for fear is trust. When children's trust in the world is shaken by frightening events, their trust in you must grow. You must talk to your children about these frightening happenings in a manner they can understand. It will be harder for kids to trust that the world is reasonably safe and that difficult times can be overcome if they cannot count on you to be fully available to them when they are afraid.

Don't believe the falsehood that by ignoring or giving short shrift to the scary events happening in today's world, that you are protecting your kids or prolonging their innocence. *They've heard the news already. Their friends and classmates are talking about it and television provides them with the disturbing images.*

Don't believe the falsehood that your children will brush off these worries with just one or two pep talks from you. When I ask children if they talk about these scary events with friends and schoolmates, most say that they do—and that the conversations occur often. When I ask parents if they think that their children worry about the state of the world, most say that that their kids are too preoccupied with normal everyday events. Evidently, parents see what they want to see but the truth is something else entirely.

Only you—the parents and grandparents, teachers, pastors, and scout leaders—can help our children, comprehend what is happening in today's world and show them that life, while cold and frightening at times, is also warm, loving, and meant to be fully lived.

The Good News

While life's tragedies remind us that we often have little say over how long we live, we have much to say over how *deeply* we live. Life can be rich and meaningful, however abruptly it is ended. One sure way to a meaningful life, a life with depth, is to forge a relationship with our children that are sturdier than steel—a relationship that is threaded with love and devotion and one that transcends time and mortality.

It is natural to want to protect children from upsetting events. But it is also the job of loving parents or caretakers to be available when sad or horrific things happen; to explain what can be explained; to share feelings and offer comfort; and reassure children that they will be protected, that they are loved, that God exists and loves them, too, and that their futures can still be something wonderful. **And these conversations must not be a one-time deal. They must happen often as new events unfold and the children advance developmentally.** An answer that is reassuring and sufficient to an eight-year-old probably won't satisfy a teenager.

But there is good news. Talking to your kids about the scary events in today's world will provide many positive benefits—benefits not always obvious or immediate:

- Your kids will feel safer and reassured, at least as well as can be expected.

- They will know that their feelings make sense to someone, even if they don't fully understand them themselves.

- They will view you as someone they can trust their feelings with.

- They will want to talk to you about other important events in their lives.

- They will learn more about the virtues of compassion, courage, love, and sacrifice.

- You will give them hope that upsetting or tragic events can be handled and that they can act in ways that give them a better sense of control over their lives.

- You will more fully appreciate that your value to them is not primarily as breadwinner or housekeeper, but as a teacher of virtues, a soother of feelings, and a nurturer of their spirit.

Good Intentions—Not So Good Results

No one enjoys talking to kids about sad or frightening topics. Some well-intentioned parents overwhelm the child—in the name of honesty—with gruesome facts and fears of future disasters. The child, instead of being comforted and reassured, is petrified.

More commonly, well-intentioned parents skip over the conversations altogether or make them too brief to be effective. In fact, conversations that are rushed through may have negative effects: children will sense that the grown-ups are uncomfortable and will have no choice but to talk to some other person or grapple with the anxiety and confusion on their own. Parents, in order to justify not carrying on such a conversation, tell themselves that children are too young to understand (or that teenagers are old enough to make sense of it without help). The biggest reasons parents have for avoiding or restricting discussions about the scary world we live in are:

- **Fear of making kids more upset:** As this book will show, effective conversations have a more calming effect on children, even when real and horrific facts are mentioned. Research is clear that when people *talk* about upsetting events, they are more likely to get some relief and eventually heal than if they spent the same amount of time simply *thinking* about the events.

- **Fear of saying the wrong thing:** Yes, there are wrong ways to talk to kids about scary and sad topics. But there are also also right ways and this book will show you what they are. Furthermore, a caring parent can always go back to a child and correct past conversational mistakes.

- **Fear of getting too emotional themselves:** Parents may believe that if they get too emotional they will scare the children. Or they will feel embarrassed or weak by displaying painful feelings. While children will be concerned if they see a parent crying or upset, it helps them to know that these emotions are normal. A parent is still able to offer comfort and reassurance to a child during these moments. After my father died, I remember holding my ten-year-old son, Luke, and crying. The message I sent was not one of weakness or anxiety but rather, "I miss my father and you miss your grandfather. Wasn't he great?"

- **Fear of talking about death or the fact that we all will die someday:** Life's tragedies do bring home the point that none of us will live forever. Children see dead animals in the street and most kids will grieve the loss of a pet or a grandparent or other loved one at some point during their childhood. Hiding from that kind of discussion does nothing to help children feel comforted.

- **The belief that kids are ignorant about what is happening in the world:** This is wishful thinking. Children notice when adults are worried and they pay attention to that. They observe when Mom and Dad are glued to the television set, watching the latest shocking news events. They overhear words like *war, evil, death, plane crash, terrorists, gas masks, "kill Americans," bomb, shooting,* and they can't help but see some of the frightening pictures on television. Even if a parent tries to keep the information away from the kids, parents cannot control what the kids are hearing from other adults (teachers, clergy, scout leaders, grandparents, neighbors) and from other children.

    Kids are not ignorant about what is happening in the world. But they may be misinformed or unnecessarily frightened. *Don't assume that your child will approach you about his or her fears.* Even normally inquisitive and open children may keep some feelings to themselves, especially if they believe that the world situation is unchangeable or that disaster is inescapable. Go and talk to them. It is your job. It is not their job to come to you.

- **The belief that children cannot handle bad or disturbing news or that older teens can handle it by themselves:** Children will take their cue from the grown-ups. If the adults discuss the situation using the right words and offering reasonable reassurances, the children will understand and be comforted. Teenagers may be brighter and more sophisticated about the ways of the world than in previous generations but they are still teenagers—they need guidance and consolation and the courage to face the adult world that is fast approaching. That happens best when parents take an active role in their lives and make efforts to have meaningful conversations.

When the world is a scary place, what you say to your kids and how you say it can make the difference between trust or mistrust, anxiety or confidence, healing or hurting, and intimacy or isolation.

What is the best setting to talk to my kids about troubling issues? Should we talk at the dining room table over dinner? Is a chat before bedtime a good idea or would that make them too nervous before sleep?

Any setting can work as long as you or your children are not going to be distracted and there is sufficient time. I would not begin a discussion about a serious or scary topic just before bedtime—but your child might. If so, don't be hasty. Quick answers are not always reassuring if it looks like you are trying to end the conversation quickly. If you do have a talk at bedtime, make sure you convey a sense that "We will get through this" or "You are safe" or some other reassuring comment. And say that you will discuss it further the next day if the hour is getting late.

Talking during dinner has the advantage of having a captive audience and members get a chance to hear from everybody. Similarly, talking while driving in the car together can have the same advantage. Some topics might be so pressing (the death of a loved one, some shocking neighborhood news) that the discussion won't wait for an ideal setting. You simply want to be fully available to your child once the discussion gets going.

The setting is important but not as important as your overall approach. You want to show that you are open to having conversations, that conversations are not a waste of your time, and that you are willing to truly listen to your child's concerns without dismissing their worries as childish.

Opening Up the Communication Kit: What to Look for, What to Do, and What to Say

For the first time in my life, I don't feel like I have complete control over my children's safety. My 13-year-old is afraid of us being bombed or nuclear war, which are very adult fears.

—Mother of four, quoted in the *Poughkeepsie Journal* in the aftermath of the World Trade Center attack

Terrorist attacks are only the latest events that have alarmed us all and scared our children. Consider these facts:

- Floods, hurricanes, and tornadoes have become more frequent and severe in the last ten years. In 1991, Hurricane Andrew devastated parts of Florida. Over 125,000 homes were damaged or destroyed. Nearly 175,000 people were left temporarily homeless. Sixty percent of victims thought they would die in the hurricane. One-third of all children showed significant symptoms of posttraumatic stress.

- A study in the *Journal of the American Medical Association* revealed that 10 percent of children age six or under admitted to the emergency room in a Boston hospital had reported witnessing a shooting or stabbing.

- Nearly 40 percent of sixth, eighth, and tenth graders in New Haven, Connecticut, witnessed at least one violent crime in the past year. Almost all eighth graders knew someone who had been killed.

- Twenty-five percent of youths in Chicago have witnessed a homicide by age seventeen.

- In the late 1980s and early 1990s, according to the United Nations Children's Relief Fund, 1.5 million children were killed around the world as a result of war. Four million were disabled.

- A survey in 1994 revealed that 42 percent of youths ages nine through seventeen worried about contracting AIDS. About a third feared being injured in a car wreck and about one-quarter worried about having to fight in a war. Since the terrorist attack on America in 2001, the vast majority of Americans believe that more attacks will occur.

- According to the FBI, five out of six Americans will become victims of violent crimes during the course of their life.

You have tremendous power to help your children cope during scary and sad times. In fact, the more helpful you are, the more likely your children will develop psychological *resilience* and effectively manage their emotional reactions during future trying times. The key strategies you need to use form the mnemonic SAFE:

Search for hidden fears and concerns your children might have;

Act effectively by spending more time with your children and finding active ways for them to have creative outlets for their fears;

Feel feelings by knowing how to appropriately share your own emotions and by showing understanding and empathy for your children's feelings;

Ease minds by offering reasonable reassurances to your children that they are safe and upsetting events are being effectively managed.

Opening Up the Communication Kit

Putting the SAFE method into action is what this book is all about and will be described in more detail in the next chapter. Before you can effectively implement the SAFE approach to talking to children about frightening events, you need to broaden your knowledge in three areas:

1. **Relevant Information:** The signs and symptoms to look for in kids affected by worry or trauma, and the concerns that most children have even if they appear untouched by fear

2. **Meaningful Action:** Steps to take that will spur on communication and emotional healing.

3. **Effective Words:** Specific words, phrases, questions, and answers to use in your discussions that will promote more dialogue, calm irrational fears, and instill hope

Opening Up the Communication Kit: Step One
RELEVANT INFORMATION:
KNOW WHAT TO LOOK FOR AND EXPECT

Mary's mom works in the post office. When Mary learned that anthrax had been mailed to many people across the country, she worried about her mother's safety. She displayed a reluctance to attend school because it meant saying good-bye to her mom. Occasionally she had nightmares.

Jim was in the sixth grade. His life seemed routine despite world events. He attended school every day and played with his friends. Sometimes they would discuss the war on terrorism. His parents were divorced and he didn't discuss terrorism with them.

Cindy's older brother enlisted in the Navy after having spoken about it for two years. At one time it seemed like an exciting career. Now, Cindy was afraid for him. What if he went to war? What if he got killed?

How well each of those children cope depends on key factors. In fact, even though events have not touched Jim personally, he could potentially have more symptoms than Mary or Cindy, depending on his temperament and the involvement of his parents and family in his life.

CHILDREN AT RISK FOR SYMPTOMS

A person's reactions to traumatic or scary events can vary depending upon four main factors:

1. Intensity of the current threat and the number of previous times his or her sense of safety has been threatened

2. Degree of personal exposure to the threat

3. Skill level in coping with problems and emotional turmoil

4. Effective and reliable support from trusted others. This may be the most crucial variable. It has been shown repeatedly that the parent–child relationship is a key factor in development of resilience and the ability to cope in children.

Threats of bodily injury or possible death are very intense and can cause symptoms to emerge after the event has passed. Children who have suffered past traumas such as abuse, who are grieving the loss of a parent or pet or loved one, who have had trouble learning in school, or who have had behavioral problems, may show more signs of stress than kids without such experiences.

Children whose homes are severely damaged in a hurricane, who survive a near fatal accident, who were in a school when a shooting occurred, or who witnessed violence first hand are more at risk for symptoms than children who watch these events on television.

Children who fluster more easily, who are either more aggressive or withdrawn, or who seem less effective at managing their emotions than their peers may show more signs of agitation or fear during difficult times.

Children who cannot count on their parents or family for regular, effective emotional support (perhaps there are problems in the family such as alcoholism, frequent fighting, or marital disruptions) are at greater risk for symptoms than are kids with solid, reliable emotional support. Research findings suggest that children are likely to be more resilient when child-rearing strategies combine emotional warmth with clear, structured rules and reliable enforcement of those rules. Warmth without structure is too permissive. Structure without warmth is too militaristic and invites either defiance or total submission.

KINDS OF SYMPTOMS

After a tragedy, loss, or disturbing event, children may exhibit one or more of many symptoms. Children who experience trauma or loss first hand may not develop symptoms right away. A delayed onset is not unusual so parents must not presume that the absence of obvious symptoms means that a child is unaffected.

Neither is it necessary for the child to have experienced the trauma first hand for symptoms to appear. A major event that is upsetting to adults or that causes a large upset in routines for the family, community, or nation (such as the terrorist attack upon New York City and Washington, D.C.) can create heightened stress in children of all ages.

Common symptoms include:

Worry and fears about future threats to safety. *Will it happen again? What will happen next? Am I in danger or are you?* are common concerns. Deeper fears include fear of separation from loved ones and fear of injury or death to oneself or one's family.

Nightmares and disturbed sleep. A child may have a hard time getting to sleep or will awaken often. It is a good idea to spend extra time with the child at bedtime and provide additional comfort such as longer bedtime stories, snuggling, lights on during sleep, finding a special stuffed animal, and so forth. If the child is having a particularly difficult time (extra clingy, panicky, unrelenting fears), allowing the child to sleep with you or with a sibling temporarily is perfectly acceptable and probably a good idea. Unless the child is traumatized, you can wean him or her back to the normal sleeping routine often within a week. Some children may take longer before they resume their normal sleep pattern.

Physical complaints especially stomachaches and headaches and vague concerns about "not feeling well." These complaints are not imaginary. They could be due to real medical conditions or, more likely, are stress related. Stress-related symptoms tend to subside when the child is offered extra doses of reassurance, comfort, and time with a trusted loved one such as a parent or grandparent. Observe your child from a distance to see when he or she starts to resume more normal types of play behavior or otherwise seems to feel better. If you are concerned that over-rewarding your child may actually reinforce "sick" behavior, you can offer more special moments together *after* the child does some chores, homework, or finishes a meal.

Regressive behaviors such as bedwetting, thumb sucking, tantrums, separation anxiety, or clinging. Teenagers may become (even more) irritable or defiant. Old phobias that had been overcome may reappear (monsters under the bed, animals, and strangers). Don't lecture or scold or otherwise shame a child who acts in these ways. They are not being willfully difficult. They are scared, feeling helpless, and unable to put events into a helpful perspective. Be consoling, soft, more attentive, reassuring, and interject some fun and humor when appropriate.

Withdrawal from family routines or being more quiet and noncommunicative than usual. Don't assume that your child is working it out in his or her own way and is better off left alone. Try to draw him or her out whenever possible (read Chapter 10 for detailed guidelines) and show that you are *always* approachable and interested in talking.

Less-communicative kids have a knack for opening up at inopportune times. No matter how busy you are at the moment, drop everything and let them see that you are very interested in what they have to say.

Strong startle response. Children in war zones may scream at the sound of an airplane or a firecracker. A popping balloon may cause sudden fear in kids who witnessed a shooting. Abused children may jump when someone unexpectedly touches them.

Repetitive play is one way young children deal with a disturbing event. Using dolls or toy soldiers or puppets (or by drawing or coloring), a child may reenact a traumatic or upsetting event. It is a sign that the youngster was indeed troubled by what happened. If the reenactments decline in frequency, it is one indication that the child is coming to terms with what happened. Parents may want to use repetitive play as a cue to talk with their child. It might be helpful to play with the child but change the outcome of the traumatic event to something that is realistic and positive. For example, a child injured in an auto accident who uses toy cars to reenact a car crash, might be guided to enact a scene where the injured people learn to drive in cars without fear or subsequent injury. Speak for the dolls and say things like, "Car accidents do happen but not very often . . . It was scary but I came through it okay . . . I have many memories of fun times while driving in a car. . . ."

TIMING OF SYMPTOMS

Parts two, three, and four of this book guide readers through the three main phases of stress and show how to answer difficult questions children may ask and how to maximize conversational effectiveness.

Briefly, the initial phase of trauma might be called the *Worry Phase* because anxiety often begins here. In this phase, people witness, hear about, or participate in some frightening, traumatic event and experience a strong rush of fear, anxiety, and perhaps shock. They may cry hysterically, they may be unable to calm down and are clearly preoccupied with the disturbing events. They may seem frozen in fear. Children may have a difficult time comprehending what happened to them because they simply have not lived long enough to realize that certain bad things can and do occur. Remember that for very traumatic events (sexual abuse, kidnapping, a terrifying house fire, and so on) a child might develop symptoms weeks or months after the trauma has passed.

The second phase I call the *Work Phase*. The traumatic event is now over, the person is clearly safe and out of immediate danger, but the memory of the event and the fear of future calamity is strong. During this phase people try to get on with their lives as best as they know how but are on edge and may suffer symptoms of stress such as sleep disturbances, concentration problems, irritability, and irrational fears. This is the phase where parents may see their children resume thumb sucking or bedwetting. *Just because a child is able to go to school or play with friends and function normally does not mean he or she is no longer troubled by what happened.* Kids often cope with intense emotions in waves. It is common, for example, for a child whose parent recently died to be crying or withdrawn one minute and jumping rope the next.

The final *Well-being Phase* occurs when troubling symptoms have disappeared and the person feels a sense of reasonable confidence that his or her world is safe and predictable. Kids at this phase demonstrate age appropriate emotions and behaviors and report that the memory of the event no longer troubles them like it once did. They will not get to this point unless a trusted adult—usually a parent—has been available to them for conversation, reassurance, and shared regular activities.

Opening Up the Communication Kit: Step Two
MEANINGFUL ACTION: KNOWING WHAT TO DO.

Effective communication with kids during scary times relies on action not just words. The action steps you take can set the stage for meaningful, helpful dialogue with your children or, conversely, will interfere with effective dialogue.

Be there physically. Make sure you spend more time with your child after a traumatic or disturbing event. Even if your child only witnessed it on television, the more scary and intense the event, the more likely your child needs more comfort and reassurance than is obvious. Do a few more activities together, read at bedtime, and help out at bath time even if you usually let your spouse do that. Play catch, play tag, put puzzles together, horse around, and go for a walk.

Show a lot of affection. If you are not the affectionate type, do it anyway. Your discomfort with affection is not as important as a child's emotional well-being. According to the book, *Talking to Children about Nuclear War* by psychologist William Van Ornum, many loving parents freeze up when talking to their children about scary issues. Frightened themselves by the prospect of nuclear war or global terrorism, these parents sometimes forget to put an arm around their kids or touch them reassuringly during discussions.

Don't let your children watch the TV news alone. Don't let them watch it often. Children age four or five may see a tragic scene replayed on television, such as the planes crashing into the World Trade Center, and not understand that it is the same event being reshown. Instead, they think that many buildings in many places are being attacked. You need to be there to ask and answer questions and to make sure your child understands what you want him or her to understand.

Resume normal routines as soon as possible. Children are reassured by familiar routines: Daddy making breakfast, attending school, going to the supermarket or shopping mall, playing with kids in the neighborhood or with favorite video games, Mom's unbeatable brownies, the ride to Grandma's house, church on Sunday.

Talk to school officials and teachers (as well as scout leaders, coaches, babysitters and anyone else your child sees regularly) about their policies on addressing the scary news of the world. This is your chance to alert teachers to any concerns you have about your child's emotional state, or to be alerted by teachers. Find out if your child is acting differently. A child who is grieving the loss of a loved one might not perform as well in school. If the loved one died unexpectedly or in some gruesome accident, children can be especially upset.

Be patient with your kids. Cut your partner some slack. Be as understanding as possible that other family members may be out of sorts. When your nerves are frayed, children may act up or simply demand their usual amount of attention. Grouchiness is understandable but do your best to rise above it. Children upset by world events will take their cue from you on how to act and how to feel. An extra jittery, rambunctious, or irritable child may simply be charged up because you have yet to act as a circuit breaker to the flood of emotions the family is feeling.

Exercise. Try to have some relaxation time. Talk to other adults to help you sort out and reduce your own anxieties. Do something to reduce your own nervous energy. Put aside some low priority chores and make sure you have some quality and quantity time with your partner as well as recuperative time for yourself. Sure you're busy. But a little rest and relaxation will go a long way right now. Your kids may thank you for it.

Attend religious services regularly. Make sure your kids attend, too. People who pray and attend services cope better during difficult times. If you've wanted to attend more often but hadn't gotten around to it, there is no better time than when your family, your community, or your nation needs your prayers. Spirituality has made a comeback since the 9/11 tragedy. People find that religion not only brings them closer to God but closer to their neighbors and community.

Get your children to do something positive and helpful for others. Remind your kids to pray for victims and pray for peace. Have them visit a local police or fire department and drop off a thank-you letter or drawing. Help them come up with ideas for raising money for charities. Teach them that hardship and tragedy is a time for all people to come together and help one another.

Get along better with your ex-spouse. Whether you are married, separated, or divorced, your children need support from both of their parents. Even happy marriages can be strained when the stress of world events raises fears about the economy and personal safety. If you are divorced, tell your ex what questions the kids have been asking about war or terrorism or school safety. Let him or her know how you responded. If you disagree on how to talk to the kids about their fears, remind one another that you both have good intentions, that reasonable people may disagree, and try to find some kind of common ground. Say thanks if the conversation goes well and your ex is supportive.

Opening Up the Communication Kit: Step Three
EFFECTIVE WORDS: KNOWING WHAT TO SAY.

The remainder of this book provides specific and flexible examples of what to say and what not to say to children during scary times. But important *general* guidelines need to be mentioned here.

Search for your child's hidden concerns or fears (the *S* in SAFE). Many kids will not verbalize what's bothering them. Some kids may want to talk but do not know how to express what they are experiencing. Children watching footage of bombing raids on television may worry that bombing could occur in their community. A child whose parent works in a tall building may secretly worry that the building will be a target of terrorism. A child involved in a scary event such as abuse or car accident may feel secretly responsible for what happened. If a child expresses concern or sympathy for a victim, you might want to probe to see if he or she is worried about personal safety. "You seem worried about those kids on TV who lost their homes in a flood. Do you worry that the same thing could happen to us?"

Feel feelings (the *F* in SAFE). Let your children know that their feeling reactions are normal. Help them to manage their emotions. Emotions tend to calm down when we know we are listened to and understood. Telling a child there is no need to cry or to worry when he or she is feeling very frightened is like telling a child who hasn't eaten in eight hours that he really doesn't feel hungry. It is a dismissive, confusing message to a child who then learns that feelings don't make sense and that expressing emotion is the wrong thing to do. You want your children to trust that they can come to you when they are emotionally troubled.

When anthrax first made the headlines, Vice-President Cheney stated that a more debilitating problem was the *fear* of anthrax. In other words, it is not just an event that creates problems for us. Our emotional reaction to the problem can create more stress and upheaval or less, depending on how well we manage those emotions.

Ease minds (the *E* in SAFE). Explain why you think your child is safe (or reasonably safe). Don't limit your comments to things like, "You have nothing to worry about . . . There's no reason to be concerned." Well-intentioned efforts to reassure children they are safe can backfire if adults sound dismissive or insincere. Some adults may actually be sending the message, "That's a stupid question . . . You don't need to ask about this anymore . . . I don't want to discuss it."

Say things like, "I wouldn't let you go to school if I thought you were in danger . . . Many kids feel nervous and afraid but I believe our family is safe . . . Bad things do happen to people but fortunately they happen very rarely to most of us."

Feel and express your feelings, but don't overwhelm children with anxiety in the name of being "open and honest" with them. I was interviewed on a radio program two weeks after the World Trade Center was destroyed. A woman caller stated that when her seven-year-old daughter asked if her Midwest town would be blown up, the woman answered (shockingly), "Yes, it's possible." The woman defended her comment by saying she could never in a million years lie to her daughter and that she had no way of knowing if her town would one day be blown up or not.

That mother was wrong to have said that. Just like a child who touches a hot, ungrounded electrical wire will get shocked, a child who listens to a distraught, unthinking (ungrounded) parent will get a jolt of fear. Parents must act as emotional circuit breakers. Denying their feelings to the kids probably won't work since kids are adept at reading between the lines. Better to express some degree of concern while at the same time easing the child's mind. For example, "The anthrax threat concerns me but I'm not worried that I or anyone else I know will get the disease. In fact, it is very treatable even for people who get it . . . Yes, bomb threats do happen but I'm not worried at all for your safety. If I was worried, you can be sure I would do everything I could to protect you."

Don't lecture. Lengthy explanations usually are not necessary and often are a sign that you are not listening as effectively or as often as you should to your child. Older kids may decide not to ask you important questions if they anticipate a speech or a history or geography lesson.

Don't presume to have all the answers. You are not a walking encyclopedia. You don't need to know the chemical make-up of anthrax or the capital of Afghanistan. If your child asks an important question such as "What is the principal doing to make sure my school is safe?" and you don't know the answer, say "I don't know. But I'll find out." If your child asks more scary questions like, "Will you die in a terrorist attack?" reassure him or her that you have every expectation of living a long life.

Initiate a discussion about a recent scary event. Help your child discuss it. Encourage expression of thoughts and feelings. Say, "Tell me more . . . What else? . . . What are your friends saying about this? . . . What worries do you have?" Help younger kids identify the feelings they are expressing. "It sounds like you are feeling mad (sad, scared, and so on)."

If my child shows none of the signs that he is distressed by recent world events is it reasonable for me to avoid any lengthy or serious discussions? I don't want to make him unnecessarily upset. I remember when my father died, he was a little upset but not very much. When would conversations about painful or scary topics be unnecessary?

I encourage parents and other caretakers to probe for underlying concerns a child might have but may not be exhibiting. If you knew that your son went to bed at night worried about the future of the world, I'm sure you would want to talk with him and reassure him. Many kids have secret worries that they don't bring up but that don't seem to hinder their day to day life. But still those worries exist. Saying something like, "Some kids your age might worry about _____. Do you ever feel that way, even a little?" might spark an interesting conversation. If probing doesn't result in any new information and your child seems to be doing fine, then you probably don't need to push the topic any further. But most parents err on the side of saying too little to their kids instead of saying too much. Consequently, they miss opportunities for conversations when their kids are, in fact, troubled by something.

Even if a child shows no significant distress—such as when your father died—you can still invite discussions without being pushy. You can speculate aloud as to what your child might be feeling. "I wonder if you are feeling _____?" Sometimes that helps prod a child into a discussion. Pull back if your efforts don't get any results.

The SAFE
Approach to
Effective
Communication

3

I think we should live life to the fullest. It might end anytime.

—Nicole B., age 13, watching news clips of the bombing of Afghanistan by the United States

You never know when your plane will leave to go to heaven.

—Lea C., age 13

Children aren't just thinking about the short term. It is normal for kids everywhere to wonder such things as *What will I be when I grow up? Will I get married? What will my husband or wife look like?* So it isn't surprising that these days many children wonder if they will have to always be on guard for future danger or if they will have to fight in a war. When terror hits close to home as it does when residents of a city absorb the shocking news of a local anthrax infection or when children have to practice school safety drills for bomb threats and shootings, kids may think about something they never thought much about before: dying young.

Children may or may not express those worrisome thoughts. And if they do speak up, they are likely to be told there is no need to worry and not to think such things. If they don't mention it again, parents will assume it has been forgotten.

When the world has become a scary place for kids, parents need to provide them with more than pat answers or hasty reassurances. Conversations need not be lengthy. Parents should initiate the dialogues but always be willing to respond with interest whenever a child raises any concerns or questions.

There is no cookbook formula for speaking to kids about scary or sad topics, nor should there be. Parents need to tailor their comments to meet their own children's particular needs and the family's situation. However, there are key elements that should always be kept in mind. They form the mnemonic SAFE:

Search. Probe for hidden concerns your child may have;

Act. Have your child act in ways that will be helpful to those in need or that will provide a normal structure to his or her day;

Feel feelings. Let your child express strong or painful emotions. Share your feelings, too, but don't overwhelm your child.

Ease minds. Provide realistic reassurances of safety and frequent reassurances of love.

At least two of these elements—if not all four—will be required in most conversations for the child to come away properly informed and feeling safe. Well-meaning parents often overlook or misapply at least one of the SAFE elements.

Search for Hidden Concerns

The *S* in SAFE stands for search. Many children will ask questions that contain a hidden question. For example, *What is anthrax?* is really a question that asks, *Am I (or are you) in danger?* (a common hidden concern). *Will there be another war?* is not just a curiosity. Your child is worried about his or her future and may even envision enemy soldiers in your driveway. *Why did it happen?* may also mean *Will it happen again?* If you respond only to the question asked, you may miss an opportunity for a more helpful discussion.

Probe for hidden meanings. Ask questions that will get your child to tell you more information.

- That's an interesting question. What made you think of it?
- I just gave you the answer but maybe you have other questions, too.
- What else is on your mind about this?
- I wonder if you have some worries that you haven't mentioned yet?
- I haven't asked you about ＿＿＿＿ in a while. What new thoughts or feelings do you have about it?

- What are kids in school worried about these days?
- Do you sometimes have questions that worry you but haven't had time to talk to me about?
- Before _____ happened, what was your biggest worry? What is your biggest worry now?
- You ask that question a lot. I'm glad you asked it again because it must really be on your mind. (Don't express annoyance when your child asks the same questions over and over. An overly worried child is apt to do that.)
- The radio newscaster just gave the latest report. Tell me what you thought about it.

If your child displays an emotion (or you believe your child is experiencing an emotion) ask about it.

- You seem worried by my answer. What might be worrying you?
- I answered your question but you still look concerned. What else is on your mind?
- Sometimes people watching TV feel bad for the victims they see. Do you feel like that? What goes through your mind when you see that on TV?
- You seem to be upset (cranky, irritable, mad, quiet) a lot lately. I'm thinking something is bothering you. I'd like to hear what it is.
- A lot of kids your age worry about future terrorism (shootings, and so on). What worries do you ever have about that?

- I gave you that answer already. Why do you keep asking the same questions? (Don't discourage communication. It is normal for kids to repeat questions.)
- We'll have to talk about it later. (Take the time now. It may only take a minute or two. Let your child know that his or her concerns are uppermost on your mind. If you need to end the discussion, say "This is important and I'm glad we're talking about this. Is it okay if I mention it later? I have to get to work now.")

Take Action

The *A* in SAFE stands for Action. Children will probably feel better (as will adults) if their normal daily routine is not drastically altered. Getting kids to do their homework, play ball, and clean their rooms lets them know that life is still predictable (and therefore reasonably safe). Even better, help them to find a way to reach out to someone else who might appreciate a visit, or a gift such as a drawing, or a kind word. Such actions not only teach compassion and kindness, but it gives the child a sense of influence over events. Helplessness in the face of tragedy or terror makes the situation worse. Knowing we can do something that will make us feel a little better or that will be helpful to another person actually improves our sense of coping and reduces stress.

Remind children of the normal activities you expect them to participate in. In the days or weeks following a major disturbing event, you may want to spend time with them doing some of those activities.

- Time to do your homework. I'll go over it with you.

- Let's tidy up your bedroom. I'll help.

- I need to get gasoline for the lawnmower. Want to ride with me to the gas station?

- We'll be visiting Grandma this weekend.

- How about I read you a story tonight?

- Let's turn off the TV and play a game.

- I'm thinking of getting tickets for the ballgame. Do you like that idea?

Suggest ways that your child can help others.

- If a friend of yours is scared, you can talk to him. That might make him feel better.

- How about you draw a picture and we drop it off at the firehouse? The firefighters would really like it, I'm sure.

- Would you like to earn some extra money to donate to those people who need our help?

- Want to help me make a casserole for Mrs. Jones? She's feeling very sad these days. She might like some company, too.

- Find something to do. (This sounds dismissive. Help your child with ideas on what to do.)

- Just keep busy and try to forget about upsetting things. (Yes, keeping busy may take a child's mind off of disturbing events—and that is beneficial. But you are giving the message that thinking about upsetting things is wrong. Better: "Sometimes, when you don't want to think or talk about upsetting things, it helps to stay busy.")

Feel Feelings

The *F* in SAFE stands for feel feelings. Many parents are uncomfortable with strong emotions—either their own or their children's. Some (men more than women) find it hard to be good listeners or offer tender words of encouragement. Instead they try to talk their children out of their feelings. Kids who are scared or grieving need to know they can express their feelings and be understood. *That* makes them feel better. Don't forget to hug, hold, or touch your child when discussing painful emotions.

Correct any misconceptions they have but don't tell them they are wrong to feel the way they do. Young children may not be able to even identify the emotion they are feeling. They need you to label it for them.

- I don't blame you for feeling that way.

- I feel sad (angry, scared, and so on), too. That's normal. But it won't last.

- You are thinking about what you saw on television and it worries you. Do I have that right?

- You may be feeling scared about _____.

- What else are you feeling? Some kids your age feel _____.

- When somebody has an upset stomach or a headache it can sometimes be due to worry. Is there something you are worried about that we can discuss?

- Sometimes when a person is cranky or in a bad mood, they are unhappy or concerned about something. Today you seemed to be a bit cranky. Is something worrying you or making you mad?

- Don't feel sad.
- Don't feel bad.
- Don't feel mad.
- Don't feel scared.
- There's no need to feel that way.
- Big boys (girls) don't get upset about these things.
- Mommy (Daddy, Grandma, and so on) wouldn't want you to feel this way.
- You're acting like a baby.
- Have a cookie, you'll feel better.
- You'll feel better soon. (This is good to say. It is reassuring. But if said without some discussion or probing, the child might think you'd rather not talk. *Better:* "Yes, it was scary when the kids had to evacuate the school because of the bomb threat. It's normal to feel scared about that. But I know you'll feel better soon.")

Ease Minds

The E in SAFE stands for ease minds. Should you ease a child's mind immediately? Yes, if the child is worried about personal safety or the safety of friends or loved ones and safety can be reasonably expected. But if you are not careful, hasty reassurances can send the message, *Let's not talk any more about this,* and may shut down further discussion. Sometimes, reassurances are best given only *after* the listener has understood the child's feelings.

When bad things happen and the world is a scary place, kids need reassurances that they (and loved ones) are safe and that adults are taking steps to insure future safety.

- Yes, bad things can happen unexpectedly. But I would not let you go to your school (the mall, on a train, and so on) if I thought you'd be in danger.
- What happened to you was very frightening. But it's over now and you are safe.
- Yes, I get a little scared when these awful things happen. But I believe the future will be happy for us.

- I believe that the President and the government are doing a good job protecting us all from future harm.
- The person that did this to you will never come near you again.
- Kids who are very frightened might take a while before they feel safe. But they will feel safe and you will, too.
- We are doing all we can to stay safe and live a normal life. Yes, bad things sometimes happen but very rarely. I believe we are safe from harm and I'm enjoying every day.
- Yes, Uncle Pete is a firefighter and that can be dangerous work. But he learned how to be very careful and has been safe so far. Even if he gets hurt one day he will almost certainly get better.
- Some people are at risk for danger but I don't believe we are. These are my reasons. . . .
- The postal workers check all the mail and we know what to look for. We have strong medicines that help people with anthrax.
- Other people are going through what we're going through. They'll get through it and so will we.

How Not to Say It

- Don't be silly. There's nothing to worry about. (Too dismissive.)
- I told you before we'll be fine. Stop bringing that up.
- Don't believe everything you see on TV.

Sometimes, knowing that they cannot fully guarantee a child's future safety, parents give reassurances that are only partly comforting. It can be a fine line to walk, but try not to give half-comforting reassurances to children under twelve. It is true that you cannot guarantee anyone's future safety, but younger kids deserve the strongest reassurances you can give without sounding unbelievable.

- **Comforting:** All the tall buildings are checked and we believe they are safe.
  Half-Comforting: Some buildings are more at risk for attack than others are. We're trying to make sure they are all safe but we can't protect every building all of the time.
- **Comforting:** The terrorists took us by surprise the first time. Now we are looking for them and we will not be surprised.

Half-Comforting: They will surprise us again and some people will get hurt or die. But our country is fighting back.

- **Comforting:** I believe the plane we're on is safe. The people in charge know what to do to make sure it is safe.

  Half-Comforting: The plane is probably safe. We can never be absolutely sure.

- **Comforting:** I'm here with you. I'll be here to protect you if you ever need protection. I'm not going to die for a long, long time.

  Half-Comforting: I will protect you if I can. I don't think I'm going to die soon but nobody can be sure about those things.

SAFE PHRASES TO USE

I love you.

I see what you mean.

That's understandable.

Many kids feel the way you do.

Good question.

Tell me more.

I'm always here for you.

Scary times don't last.

It will all work out.

We're safe.

I'm glad you brought that up.

I'll bring this up again sometime.

What you are feeling is . . .

I'm so glad we talked.

Any other questions?

I feel confident.

That's a helpful idea.

What are your friends saying?

PHRASES TO AVOID

Never mind.

That's not important.

Didn't we just talk about this?

Forget about it.

It's the end of the world.

Your imagination is running wild.

We're not as safe as we thought.

You're worrying over nothing.

I can't handle this.

Not now.

How could you think such a thing?

Nothing's wrong.

Other kids don't feel that way.

The world is in terrible danger.

Ask your mother.

Don't feel that way.

A beloved uncle is very ill and will probably die soon. My kids, ages five through twelve, are worried about him. How can I ease their minds? When should I tell the children that he is not expected to live? I know they will feel devastated.

If you know for sure that the uncle will die soon, it is best to tell the children now. If doctors consider his case to be terminal but give him many months still to live, it's okay to wait a month or two before you tell the children he will definitely die. As a general rule, if a loved one is very ill but death is uncertain, it is best to tell the kids that death is a possibility but that doctors are doing all that they can. You don't want to fall into a trap of saying "He will be fine" and then have to inform the children later that their uncle suddenly died. If a loved one is ill and could possibly die but the greater likelihood is that the person will survive, I suggest you sound encouraging and don't mention death. "Your uncle is very sick but the doctors are confident they can help him." If a child asks outright, "Will he die?" it is better to admit the possibility of death—if there is a real possibility—but to emphasize hope. "Some people with this illness do die. But we feel pretty sure he won't die."

You asked about easing your children's minds. Unfortunately, you cannot reassure them that their uncle will be fine. However, you can use this opportunity to discuss your religious beliefs. You can explain how the family will get by without the uncle and answer any questions your children might have about the future. They may be worried about your health or another family member's health. You can ease their minds in those areas.

Part
Two

The Worry Phase of Trauma, Tragedy, or Terror

I was surprised to see that nobody was home when my son and I entered the house at 9 P.M. The phone rang a minute later and I assumed it was my wife, about to tell me she was on some errand with my daughters. But the call was from an emergency room nurse. She did not give me much information, just a mildly reassuring message that my family was okay, and that there had been a car accident. I should go to the hospital as soon as possible.

On our way there, my son and I realized that we had passed an accident scene on our way home earlier. Traffic had been backed up and diverted, emergency lights from many police cars flashed and lit up the road almost like daylight. What a horrible scene, we had remarked, one of the worst I could remember seeing in a long time. With shock we now knew that the accident didn't involve strangers. It involved my wife and two young daughters.

I kept clinging to the nurse's words: "They're okay." But what did okay mean? Seriously injured but alive? Or was the nurse lying to me so I could make it to the hospital safely? I reassured my son all was fine, wondering if I'd have to take those words back later on.

The man who had smashed into the car my wife drove had been drunk. Traveling at a high rate of speed, he ran a red light and took an unexpected hard left at an intersection, colliding with oncoming traffic. He hit a second vehicle, brand-new like my wife's. Both cars were totaled. Miraculously, all victims survived with minor injuries. I was able to take my family home that night—still picking out pieces of glass from my daughters' hair and clothes—grateful they were alive.

What happened to my family happens every day to families. They are not world-shaking, headline-grabbing events. But for the families involved they can be traumatic, especially if death or serious injury results. Those family members once thought that driving was reasonably safe. Now they know better. They once thought that their odds of being a victim of a drunk driver were small. But no more.

The world becomes a scary place to children not just when bombs go off in buildings or when news reports show planes crashing, but when their own little worlds they live and play in every day become chaotic and suddenly dangerous, shattering the beliefs that they are safe.

What You Need to Know about the Worry Phase

People recover from traumatic and disturbing events by going through three phases: Worry, Work, and Well-Being. These phases overlap. The Worry Phase occurs in the aftermath of some frightening event, may be intense or mild, and can last hours, days, or weeks, depending on the severity of the incident and the kind of help available. In some cases of trauma, symptoms may not appear right away and could be delayed for weeks or months.

During the Worry Phase, people feel in shock, agitated, fearful, and preoccupied. Kids will worry and often act immature for their age. If the incident is ongoing or occurs with some frequency (such as gang violence in a neighborhood or news flashes about the latest terrorist action) people may not have time to recover before a new wave of fear hits. Even when the incident is clearly over, such as the day after some tragedy—people can still feel as if the event is still happening. They can't get it out of their heads and their levels of fear are still heightened.

Adults must start a dialogue with children during the Worry Phase even if the children do not appear troubled by what happened. Talking alleviates fear and may root out any hidden issues. What you say depends upon the child's age.

0–3 years old: Say nothing unless the child has heard about, witnessed, or participated in some upsetting event. Then, focus on the positive and give strong reassurances. Very young children will pick up on your emotions even if you keep thoughts to yourself. "That was scary. But you're safe now. . . . Everything is fine . . . Mommy's sad by what she saw on TV but she's so happy to play with you" are examples of appropriate ways of talking.

4–6 years old: These children cannot always distinguish between reality and fantasy (monsters under the bed are real to these kids). Be careful about using overly dramatic or descriptive language. They need to hear that they are loved and safe. Their fears and concerns need to be listened to, not quickly dismissed in a misguided effort to make them feel better. Hear them out, correct misunderstandings, and focus on positive events when possible. Minimize TV or radio news reports of frightening events.

The concept of death is hard to understand at this age. Kids think death is reversible. Consequently, they may ask over and over if a loved one who has died will return or come for a visit.

Young children may have no words to describe some tragedies. Children whose houses are severely damaged in a terrifying hurricane or who witness a shooting or homicide cannot easily integrate those events into their concepts of how the world works. You'll have to give them the words to help them understand.

Get them involved with normal activities that provide them with structure and familiarity. If you express your fears and worries, do so mildly and offer hope. It is perfectly okay to express strong sadness if you are grieving a loss. Just make sure that your child understands that all will eventually be okay even if you are very sad now.

7–12 years old: Kids in these middle years are very aware of what is happening around them but too young to fully comprehend. They don't think abstractly. Terms like *peace, war,* and *terrorism* are understood only at a basic level. They prefer to think in black and white terms. Things are good or bad, wrong or right, okay or not okay, safe or unsafe. There are good guys and bad guys. Children in this age range may be fascinated with the details of death and dying. They may ask questions that seem inappropriate such as, "What do the bodies under the rubble look like?" They begin to understand that death is final and will worry about who will take care of them should a parent die.

If a child in this age range senses that his or her parents are too troubled by events, the child may deny anything is wrong and not admit to worries. Parents must probe for underlying concerns these kids might have.

13–18 years old: These kids have the capacity to think abstractly and in depth and analyze details. So if a school is unsafe, why should a mall be safe? Will they be drafted as future soldiers? Teenage boys may react to horror on television like they are playing a video game. "Wow . . . cool" or they may crack jokes. Then later on have a somber discussion with friends about their underlying worries. Trite reassurances from parents that all will turn out well won't sound sincere to teenagers. Don't wait for a teenager to express worries about safety before offering reassurances—he or she may not verbalize those fears. Some teens may verbalize hostility toward other ethnic groups. Parents need to remind them that bigotry doesn't help but that the underlying feelings of anger are normal. Any acting out or decline in grades after some scary event can be expected for many teens. Don't scold them as if they are being willfully defiant. Other teens may cope by focusing on schoolwork to help them keep their mind off worries. Don't presume they are fine simply because they are studying hard. They may be frightened and need to talk.

How to Start a Conversation When Something Bad Has Happened

A hush of silence falls on us like a boulder.
We are there, hoping.

—Adam V., age 13, after the terrorist attack on the United States

When I am eighty years old and my grandchildren ask me about this war,
I will tell them the gruesome truth.

—Chelsea L., age 12, talking about terrorism

The reactions of the parents to stressful events can deeply affect the reactions of
children, especially among the youngest children.

—Kenneth Fletcher, research psychologist at the University of Massachusetts Medical School,
as quoted in the *Cape Cod Times*, October 7, 2001, p. G3.

When we are stunned by horror and tragedy words may not come easily. Then again, they may come pouring forth. In each case it will be a juggling act—trying to comprehend incoming facts, while numbed by disbelief and the heavy weights of fear, anguish, and perhaps the deep sympathy for another's loss.

If you are lucky, the scary events are far away and you and your family are safe for now. But man-made horrors can no longer be clicked off like terrifying DVD movies. Everybody is on edge. Kids are admitting that they are frightened and preoccupied. And whether it is terrorism, war, horrible accidents, abuse, or natural disasters, more and more parents and caretakers find themselves having to discuss tragedies and devastation and somehow explain the unexplainable to their children.

It would be wonderful to protect our children from horrible violence or news. But most of the time we cannot. So we have to find a way to effectively talk about these things with them.

The Worry Phase is only the first phase. Further discussions will be necessary long after the events have passed and life has returned to some degree of normality—if only to monitor how the children are doing. Initially, children will be upset and troubled by all the commotion around them—particularly if the grown-ups are distraught or in emotional shock. A child exposed to some tragedy who appears untroubled may in fact be fine, especially if the event was low intensity and involved strangers. But you won't know for sure unless you talk.

You have four tasks initially. There is no preferred order.

1. Explain the facts of what happened in basic terms.
2. Acknowledge your child's feelings (Feel feelings/Search for hidden feelings).
3. Report your own emotions.
4. Offer realistic reassurances.

You have a fifth and extremely important task, as well: explaining *why* a tragedy or disaster has happened. Guidelines for this task will be provided in the next chapter because it is important enough to deserve special attention.

EXPLAIN FACTS

Be straightforward. Use simple terms. Do not give graphic details. Probably, you will also need to offer reassurances when appropriate.

- Two planes crashed into the side of those large buildings. There was a huge fire and many people have died.
- A hurricane severely damaged the homes of thousands of people. Aunt Mary's home was damaged. She went to the hospital but she will be okay.
- Your sister was in a serious car accident. We have to go to the hospital and find out how she is doing. The doctors are taking care of her now.

- Your friend is upset because his brother is in the Army and has to fight in a war. He is worried that his brother will get hurt or killed. Maybe there are some things you can say or do that will help your friend (The *A* in SAFE is for action steps).

- Some people are getting sick by opening mail that contained very rare germs. But very few people are sick and most get better. I'm not concerned that it will happen to us.

- Some people have died from anthrax poisoning. Some bad people put those germs in letters and mailed them out. It is scary but it is also extremely rare. I'm not worried about us getting sick. If you'd like, I'll check the mail more carefully.

- A student went to school with a gun and started shooting. The news reporters are talking about it now. Some children were injured, and one died. It is very sad. The adults in charge will figure out ways to make schools safer.

ACKNOWLEDGE YOUR CHILD'S FEELINGS

Sometimes your child's feelings won't be obvious and you'll have to probe. Remember, the *F* in SAFE stands for feel feelings.

- You seem sad at the news. Am I right?

- Some kids will worry that their schools are not safe. Are you worried?

- You've been very quiet since the news. I'm thinking you might be worried or scared.

- You were looking forward to college in a few years. Now you're concerned about wars. I don't blame you.

- You've had quite an emotional day. How are you doing?

- A lot of kids your age get very sad watching the news reports. What are your thoughts about what has happened?

- Your stomach usually hurts when you are very upset and worried. Let's talk about all that's on your mind.

- Does what happened make you angry at all? People can get angry at this situation.

- You feel guilty for arguing with your dad and now he is in the hospital. All kids will get mad at their parents once in a while. He understands that and he loves you.

- You are nervous about getting on an airplane (or going into a tall building). That's normal. But planes are safer now than they have ever been. I wouldn't let you on a plane if I believed it would hurt you.

- You're scared every time I leave you. You're scared you won't see me again. Many kids feel that way but you will soon see that I'm okay. I'll call you in a little while, okay?

- It is awful to see your sister wrapped up in all those bandages. It makes us all scared and sad. But we're all so happy she's alive.

Get feedback on what you've said so far.

- Does talking about this make you feel better or worse?
- What was it I said that helped you feel better?
- Is there something I said that you wish I hadn't?
- What have your teachers (grandparents, friend's parents) said about all this? What did they say that especially helped you?
- It helped me a lot when you asked me _____.
- I liked it when you said _____.

Report Your Feelings and Offer Realistic Reassurances

Since many children will sense your feelings even if you don't speak up, it's best to clarify how you feel to eliminate misunderstandings.

Whenever possible try not to panic or act overwhelmed. Your child needs to know that you will all get through the ordeal. Out of control emotions are not reassuring.

- When I saw the pictures on TV I started to cry. It was so sad.
- It makes me angry that bad people would do this to our country.
- I feel so sorry for all the people that were hurt or killed.
- I feel sad and I want to do something to help. Maybe we can come up with some ideas together.
- I'm worried, too. But I believe things will work out eventually.
- Yes, bad things do happen and it makes me scared sometimes. But I know that most of the time everything is fine and we can expect many, many more good days to come.

- I do worry about the future. But I also have faith in our government to protect us and I have faith that God will help us, too.
- Whatever happens in this world I love you. That is what's most important to me and that will never change.

If you or your family is affected personally by some tragedy, you may be unable to give strong reassurances that all will be well.

Express hope, if possible. If the situation appears grim, offer reassurances that the family will somehow pull through these difficult times. Don't forget to hold, hug, or touch your child.

- The doctors tell us that Mom is in serious condition. Some people with her illness (injury) don't improve but some do. We still have reasons to hope she will get better.
- No, I cannot guarantee that you will never be in another car accident. But most people don't die in car accidents and most of the time we avoid accidents.
- I don't know what will happen. I'm worried but I'm also hopeful that everything will work out fine in the end.
- As far as I know your school is safe. Nobody can make sure that we are always safe from danger. But the grown-ups in charge would not let the children return to school unless we were confident it was as safe as possible.
- Let's say a prayer that everything will be okay.
- The situation has not gotten better. I'm more worried than I was but I'm still hopeful that everything will turn out all right.
- All I can be absolutely sure of right now is that I love you and will do all I can to keep you safe.

Don't give quick, incomplete answers that imply you don't want to talk. Don't be dismissive. Don't give cheery forecasts when matters are serious and grim. Don't give graphic details.

- Yes, I'm sure you heard other kids talking about it but it doesn't involve us and you don't need to discuss it. (Your child will learn not to confide in you for certain matters.)

- It's not a big deal. Everything will be fine.

- You shouldn't be watching that on TV. (If the images are frightening and involve war, terrorism, or natural disasters, your child should not watch the reports unattended. But they should be discussed, if only to find out how your child is handling the news.)

- You have no reason to be upset. (Better: The news is upsetting. Let me explain why I think we are safe.)

- It's silly to feel that way.

- There is a lot of bad news. If you get upset every time you hear bad news you'll never be happy. (Better: Bad news can make a lot of us feel sad or scared. But I've learned that most of the time good things happen to us and that we can get through the bad times and still be okay.)

- Pay no attention to your father. He always makes things sound worse than they are. (If you disagree with another adult's comments, go directly to that person and discuss it. A better comment to your child: Your dad is angry and upset over what happened. Many people feel the way he does. I'm upset, too, but I believe that we are all safe and can live our lives normally.)

- I worry that there will be a nuclear war and we will all die. (If you must bring up this concern, better to say: Nuclear war is possible but still not likely. And the government will do all it can to prevent it.)

- It was a horrible accident. The little boy's body was crushed, blood was everywhere. . . ." (Unnecessarily graphic.)

I can understand that a parent may have to explain to a child about some terrible tragedy if the child knows about it already, but I'm not sure we should inform children just for the sake of telling them information. Aren't there times when adults should stay silent and not tell kids anything?

Often, children younger than school age can be kept uninformed of certain tragedies such as school shootings or terrorist attacks. But it is hard to do that since television news is constant and the child can overhear adults and siblings discussing it. If a child sees a parent crying over some tragedy and the parent does not want to give details, it's okay to say, *"I'm just sad because some people on TV got hurt. But I'm okay and our family is okay."* A mistake well-meaning parents make is to assume that their child is uninformed or unconcerned. Often, children pick up on the nonverbal and emotional signals and may be more upset by events than is obvious. It is just a matter of time before parents will need to talk to their kids about scary events.

How to Explain to Your Child Why Bad Things Happen

5

> *There is not one child in America that doesn't know about it.*
> *Yet there is not one that understands it.*
>
> —Anna C., age 13, referring to the 9/11 attack

> *I was in denial at first, saying nothing had happened.*
> *But then I went to church and saw a little boy named Christopher*
> *crying and I truly knew that this was no joke.*
>
> —Krista F., age 15, after the 9/11 tragedy

It was April 19, 1995. Thu Nguyen heard the awful news about the bombing of the federal building in downtown Oklahoma City. His employer would not let him go by himself to the devastated site and arranged for a driver. It had only been a little while since he had dropped off his four-year-old son Christopher at the daycare center. With all the destruction that was reported, he quietly prepared himself to see the remains of his little boy in some plastic bag.

The Oklahoma City bombing took 168 innocent lives. Astoundingly, Thu's son Christopher survived despite being just twenty feet from the explosion, although he suffered severe injuries to his face. Some say that, had the boy not been in the bathroom at the time of the blast, he would have died along with many of his young friends.

Later that night the family was with Christopher in the hospital. The boy's fourteen-year-old brother could barely tolerate the sight he beheld. Christopher's face was completely bandaged, only his eyelids could be seen. Tubes snaked through his nose, his mouth, and his chest. He was so small, so fragile, and so innocent.

"Why?" the older boy kept repeating. *"Why? Why?"*

Four years later for the first time since the bombing, Christopher went with his family to the site of the explosion. A chain-link fence surrounded the area. All along the fence were posters, pictures, and letters by people who cared and wanted to share their grief, their prayers, and their heartfelt wishes of peace to the victims and the families. Pictures of the deceased were also lovingly attached to the metal links. Christopher, now age eight, glanced up and saw a photograph of a kindergarten friend who had perished. He'd not seen pictures or spoken of the boy in four years. He stared at the face and tears immediately filled his eyes.

"Why?" Christopher asked, and for days and weeks he repeated the question (which is typical for children to do). "Why did that man (Timothy McVeigh) do this? Why did my best friends die? Why did I live?"

The boy's parents did their best to explain. They gave answers that made sense and fit the facts. But in their hearts they knew that no answer to the question *Why?* could ever fully satisfy.

When young children hear about frightening national or local events and ask "Why?" they simply may be curious about the reasons certain bad things happen. They may not be looking for deep answers. If they seem scared, they may also be asking, "Will this happen again? Could it happen to me or to someone in my family?" Teenagers may be searching for more profound answers. "Why aren't adults taking better care of our community and our nation? Why do people do evil things?" Even when no answer seems good enough to an adult, children need some sort of concrete answer to "Why" so that events don't seem so random and unpredictable. As they mature they will realize that many tragic incidents are beyond rational explanation and that no answer to "Why?" may fully suffice.

The answers depend upon your children's ages.

Younger kids can be given explanations that explain the mechanics of death, war, or natural disasters without getting into the philosophical reasons. Of course, keep in mind the SAFE approach: Make sure you offer reassurances when possible and inquire about your child's feelings.

- They died because some people started a fire and the building burned.

- Your friend was killed because he was too close to the bomb and was not protected from it. It is very sad.

- Mommy was in a car accident and she had very severe injuries. The doctors could not fix the injuries and she died.

- Grandpa was old and got very sick. If he was younger he might have been able to get better but he was very old and the disease was stronger than he was.

- There are some people who hate Americans, especially the way that our leaders run our country. So they killed innocent people because of the way they feel. They are wrong to do that. I'm not worried that we will get hurt or killed, however.

- Some very bad people made the plane crash. That is why people died.

- The boys that came to school had guns. They should not have had them but they did. They were very angry and they shot some students. It was very scary. It is normal to get scared and sad when you hear about news like that.

- Some hurricanes are very large and dangerous and they come over the land where there are many people. Other hurricanes are out over the sea where there are no people. A dangerous hurricane can destroy property and sometimes injure or kill people.

- American soldiers are fighting the people who killed Americans. War is a scary thing but sometimes it is necessary in order to protect our country. I won't be fighting in a war and neither will anybody in our family. Soldiers are trained to do the fighting.

- Yes, some diseases kill people because doctors don't have a medicine yet that can cure them and make them better. But doctors are working every day to find the right medicines to help people. There are many diseases that we can cure today that we could not cure when your grandparents were your age.

You can speak to teenagers using more abstract concepts. When Thu Nguyen spoke to his fourteen-year-old son he said, "Among the many good people in the world there are evil people. Among the good fruit, there is bad. Don't let the things that are bad ruin what we have."

Teenagers and some older children may be given more involved responses. Don't expect them to be fully satisfied with your answers.

- Terrorists want to make people afraid and they want to make a mess of our economy and our way of life. They don't want us to be free. So they kill innocent people in horrible, unexpected ways to achieve their goals.

- We don't know why some people get killed and some manage to survive. It is hard to come up with reasons that make sense.

- Maybe the kids who shot their classmates gave signals that they were disturbed, but nobody picked up on those signals. Now teachers and parents are trying to become more aware of warning signs so they can prevent future tragedies.

- I don't think that Dad was chosen by fate to be in a car accident. He just happened to be driving his car when a drunk driver was on the road. It is scary to realize that even when we take precautions and drive safely, a bad accident can happen. But that is unusual. Most of the time we all get to our destinations safely.

- I don't know why. But I'll try to give you the best answer I can.

Ask questions to uncover additional, perhaps unstated, concerns. (The "S" in SAFE stands for search.)

- What do you think of the answer that I just gave you?

- Does my answer make you sad? (angry? worried? relieved?)

- Had you been thinking about your question for a while or did you just think of it now? Was it on your mind the past few days? It must have made you feel a little down.

- If you could say something to the people who hurt and killed the others, what would you say?

- If you could say something to a person who was injured by a terrorist, what would you say?

- Do you and your brother (sister, friends) ever talk about this stuff? What kinds of things do you tell each other?

How Not to Say It

- I already answered that question. Why do you keep asking it? (In very trying times, expect questions to be repeated by both children and adults.)

- It's not important why. (Actually, it is. People need to make sense of the world. Even though some answers may be inadequate, and there may be no clear answer to "why?" try to give a response.)

- Who knows? I try not to think about it. (This gives your child the message that it is silly to wonder why and to avoid discussions with you.)

- You ask too many questions.

- You're too young to understand.

I've tried to talk to my children about upsetting events taking place in our family and the world but my kids still seem tense and our conversations feel strained. No matter what I say it doesn't make a big difference. Am I doing something wrong?

If some loss, trauma, or tragedy personally affected the family, it can simply take time for all members to adjust and be open to conversation. Conversation aids the healing process but healing takes time. It is important to be patient and show affection to your children and to let them understand that talking helps. Also, make sure that you have been getting any support you need. If you are feeling overwhelmed, it can be more difficult to talk to the children as effectively as you would like.

You may be trying too hard. Don't try to solve everyone's problems and don't conclude that just because a child is distressed you must be doing something wrong. Some distress is normal for a given situation and cannot be avoided. I suggest that when you have conversations with your kids, that you not be so quick to talk them out of their feelings. Hear them out. Don't immediately tell them "Don't feel that way!" Offer reassurances, if possible, that the family will get through the difficult time even if you don't know how long it will take.

Some families are already at a disadvantage for coping with trauma, grief, or frightening events. Families where there is already a lot of tension or fighting, families that tend to blame one another when things go wrong rather than look for solutions, or families where there is alcoholism or substance abuse will not cope as well when adversity strikes. Family counseling with an experienced clinician can do wonders.

Responding to a Child's Initial Fears and Worries

6

It scares me. I try not to think about it.

—Julia C., age 11, talking about terrorism

When children like Julia admit that they try not to think about frightening events, they are also admitting that they do—periodically—think about those things. Many times a day or several times a week, these kids worry about past events or future happenings that no child should have to worry about.

When your child worries about scary events happening in today's world, will she come up with her own coping strategy? Will she ask you for help? Does it matter? Since a parent cannot be with a child every moment of the day, it is important for children to learn how to regulate their own emotions without always relying on adult assistance. For example, a child frightened at night by imaginary monsters may crawl into a parent's bed for comfort. Eventually, with a parent's help, the child who awakens at night with fear learns to fall back asleep on her own. She has learned to regulate her emotions—to keep them from getting out of control—and consequently feels more competent and less afraid.

Overprotective parents give the message "You need me . . . You can't cope without me" and they may undermine a child's ability to handle day-to-day problems on his own (such as by always allowing the child to sleep in a parent's bed when the child is afraid). But some parents are laid back and will intervene only if it is obvious that their child needs help. That may be of use in some situations, such as when two kids are arguing over the rules of a board game (they'll probably find a way to resolve the argument and continue their game), but is inadvisable during more fearful times.

Many children do cope well—outwardly. They play, they smile, they get good grades in school, and they have no obvious signs of distress. But recent research findings reveal that some children who seem to be coping well under adverse conditions (living in a tough, inner-city neighborhood) suffer high levels of inner distress. Some kids do not want to burden others with their worries and adults often overlook them when it comes time to offer emotional support.

The Bottom Line

When very upsetting or traumatic events occur, it is best to err on the side of being more available to your children. Don't presume that, because your children are bright, easy-going, and able to handle life's ups and downs, they are doing just fine. Do the following:

- Ask questions.
- Search for hidden concerns.
- Find out what your children are doing to cope and give additional suggestions.
- Remind them that their feelings are normal.
- Remind them that they are not alone.
- Remind them that the grown-ups are doing all they can to insure safety.
- Remind them that God is good.
- Always show affection or provide some sort of physical reassurance such as a touch or pat on the back.

A child will have immediate concerns or fears in the aftermath of some loss or tragedy. These involve safety for themselves, their family, and their friends. Common questions include:

Will it happen to me?

Other families thought that they were safe but they ended up dying. How can you be sure we'll be safe?

Mommy is a police officer (or has a dangerous job, works in a tall building). *Will she die?*

Will I have to go to war some day?
I don't want you to go to work. What if you don't come back?

It already happened to me. Could it happen again?

Answer your child's questions straightforwardly.

Will it happen to me? (Such as fears of a plane crashing, a shooting, anthrax, small pox, loss of life, or serious injury.)

0–4 years old: No. I'll make sure you are safe.

5–12 years old: It is very, very unlikely. In fact, I'm quite sure it won't happen.

13–18 years old: I wouldn't let you go on a plane (or to school) if I thought you were in real danger. As you know, no one is ever guaranteed of safety, but I believe you will be safe.

If your child responds: *How can you be sure? Other families thought that they were safe but they ended up dying.*
You reply:

- You are right. Nobody can be always sure that they are safe. Accidents do happen. Bad things happen, too. But just because something could happen does not mean that it is going to happen. It is possible that we would win ten million dollars, right? But I don't believe it will happen. Do you?

- Yes, we can never be certain we will be safe. Does that worry you?

- Many people died because they were taken by surprise. Now we know what kinds of dangers to look for and we can prevent them.

- America has had many wars but more people are alive in America than ever before. When America was a new country it was dangerous because people did not have strong medicines to help sick people. America is much safer today than it used to be.

- Other families are feeling what we are feeling. They will get through this time and so will we.

If your words say "You're safe . . . We'll be fine" but your actions say otherwise (you refuse to go on a plane or public transportation, you are obviously nervous when your child leaves for school, you won't enter large buildings or government offices, and so on), say:

- I'm nervous and scared but I know that I will feel better soon. It's like the feeling you get when you watch a scary movie—you *feel* afraid but yet you know that you are really safe at home.

- After a frightening event, it is normal for people to feel afraid even when they know they are going to be all right. I know you and I will be all right but it will take a while longer for me to not feel so afraid.

- Just because I feel afraid doesn't mean that I have something to be really afraid of. My imagination is very strong. I'm sure I'll be less afraid soon.
- Does it make you more nervous when you see that I am nervous? I don't want you to feel that way but I know I'm not helping.

Will I have to go to war one day? (This is more of a concern for teenagers, not younger children. However, younger kids might be worried about older siblings).

You reply:

- How would you feel if you had to go (if your brother or sister had to go)?
- How much do you worry about this?
- As of right now, you have to volunteer to go into the armed services. The government only drafts people if they don't have enough people. Right now they have enough, and they have had enough for many years, even though soldiers have gone to many different countries to fight or give aid.
- Even if you went into the armed services, you wouldn't automatically fight in a war.
- The war against terrorism is not like World War II or the Vietnam War. In those wars, America needed many, many soldiers. Since terrorists are few in number and they don't live in a specific country, we don't need many soldiers to fight them.

Mommy is a police officer (or, she works in a tall building). *Will she die?*

You reply:

- I can see why you would ask that question. Most kids would wonder about that. But all of the officers are well trained and can protect themselves.
- Mommy won't die. Yes, her job can be dangerous at times but she knows how to take care of herself.
- Daddy would not continue to work in that building if he believed he would die there. We believe it is safe for him to work there.

I don't want you to go to work. What if you don't come back?

You reply:

- (Search for more information.) What makes you say that? Have you worried about that before?
- Many kids will worry about that once in a while. But I plan on coming home tonight like I always do. How about if I give you a call (or send you an e-mail) later? That would be fun!

- (To a younger child) I will be back. I've come back home every day. I believe I am as safe as I have always been. If you want to keep worrying about me you can, but you don't need to because I am safe.

- (To an older child) It's normal to worry about that sometimes. But I know that I'll be home tonight and every night and that very soon you won't be so worried.

- (To an older child) I know you are old enough to realize that nobody can be certain of safety. But the truth is that most of the time we get through the day without any serious problems. The terrorists want us to feel afraid but our lives can be just as normal now as they were before.

- Thank you for being so concerned. You're a great kid. But I'm not worried and I hope that soon you won't be, either.

- Remember the time you were worried about _____ and I told you everything would turn out fine? I was right, wasn't I?

It already happened to me before. Will it happen again?

If your child experienced a trauma or loss firsthand (death of a loved one, a serious accident, witnessing violence, and so on) or if your child knows someone who experienced those events, his concerns may be more difficult to relieve. Say:

- Tell me more about what happened to you. Tell me more about what it was like for you when _____. (When children describe an upsetting experience, they may provide clues to hidden concerns or their emotional state.)

Restate the child's concern before you offer an answer. It lets the child know he was heard and it insures you understand the problem.

- You're afraid that I may have a heart attack and die suddenly because your friend's dad died suddenly. Do I have that right?

- You don't want to go in the car because of the accident we were in last week.

- You don't want to sleep upstairs because of the house fire.

- You're afraid to go into the school building because of the bomb scare yesterday.

Explain that the feelings are normal but that the risk of danger is low.

- I don't blame you for ofeeling that way. Most kids would feel like that. But I feel very healthy and my doctor told me I was fine last time I had a check-up.

- It can be a little scary to get back in a car after an accident. Let's do it in stages. First we'll just sit in the car and not go anywhere. Later we can drive just on our street. After that we can take a short trip to a place you pick out. Then we'll see how you feel. Okay?

- It's okay to sleep downstairs for a few days. Then, when you sleep back in your room I'll sit with you for a while. Remember that we also have new smoke alarms and we practiced how to get out of the house safely.

- Bomb scares are meant to make people afraid but I don't remember there ever having been a real bomb. When you talk to your friends I bet they will say they are less afraid as time goes on. For today, how about if I stop by during recess or lunch? If you'd like, I'll even take you out for lunch.

Help the child come up with his or her own ideas for coping.

- Remember when you felt worried about _____? What did you do then to feel better?

- What helps you to feel better? What have I said or done that helps a lot? What have I said or done that doesn't help much?

- Have you noticed that even when you are afraid, your fear goes away sometimes or it becomes less strong? That shows that you are coping fine.

- (Use a beloved or admired person/hero as a guide.) What would Grandpa say to you about this if he were here? What would the President tell you if you spoke to him on the phone? Do you think Michael Jordon ever feels afraid? What do you think he does to be less afraid?

PHRASES TO USE

That's normal to feel that way.	Many kids would wonder about that.
Tell me more about . . .	Good question.
Do you think about these things often?	What makes you feel better?
I feel safe.	I feel better every day about it.
You won't always feel this way.	Great idea.
Grown-ups are making it safer.	We will get the bad guys.
We aren't alone in dealing with this.	Talking to God can help.

PHRASES TO AVOID

You worry too much.   I answered that before.

Just forget about it.   That's silly.

I thought you were brave.   You're acting like a baby.

You're too sensitive.   I don't want to discuss it.

I'm very frightened.   I have enough to worry about.

If the upsetting event is over and my child seems to be doing fine, I'm reluctant to bring up the topic again. Why should I remind my child of what happened? Won't it just be upsetting? Is it really necessary?

Many children will still feel afraid from time to time though they may not mention it. If you don't bring up the topic, they may feel they are wrong to still have concerns. You need not be formal or overly serious. Say something like, *Even though it has been several weeks since _____ happened, many people feel worried or upset once in a while. Have you felt that way? Tell me more.* If children deny having concerns, let them know you may ask again in a few weeks and that you are always available for a discussion.

When Your Child Is Very Distressed (Nightmares, Acting Out, School Refusal, Intense Fears)

7

I was in the back seat when the collision happened. I saw my dad crushed behind the steering wheel. For a long time after that I'd lie in my bed at night curled up in a fetal position. I couldn't stop remembering.

Jack P., 32, recalling the emotional aftermath of his father's death twenty years ago

Oh, how it hurts like childbirth. The wounds heal slow, you just don't know.

Antwan J., age 14

Children (and adults) are more likely to suffer severe symptoms of trauma under one of three conditions:

1. They personally experience or witness some horror or life–death situation (including witnessing it on TV, which can seem very real and personal to a younger child). These are primary victims.

2. A loved one experiences some horror, and the child becomes a secondary victim, because of worry over the primary victim, or due to subsequent emotional calamity in the family.

3. The child has been a previous victim of abuse or trauma and the current situation—even if it is mild or affects strangers (such as shooting victims seen on TV)—triggers old fears.

Children can regress even if the upsetting event is not horrific. A screaming match by a married couple can prompt a seven-year-old child to suck his thumb when he had not done that in years. People of all ages can regress under stress. In an emotional crisis, mature, even-tempered adults may act confused or helpless much like a young child might act. Common stress reactions of children include bedwetting, thumb sucking, separation anxiety, nightmares, school phobia, withdrawal, or aggressive acting-out. These are signs that the child is overwhelmed and insecure. If they persist more than a month, professional help for the child or family is recommended. However long the symptoms last, parents and caretakers need to spend more time with the child, talk more about what happened, and provide reassurance that life can return to normal.

Regardless of the symptoms, help your child to talk about the upsetting events. (Younger, less-verbal children might do better to draw pictures or use puppets to recount the events.)

- Talking to me about what you saw (felt, went through) will help you to feel less scared and upset. Tell me what it was like for you.

- Tell me the first thing that happened.

- What happened next?

- If you were watching it on videotape and could stop the tape at the worst part, what would that part be?

- What part made you feel the saddest? The maddest? The most scared?

- When you think about it during the day or at night, is there a certain part that you think about more than any other part?

    If the child is distressed when recounting the story of what happened or discussing feelings, don't automatically discourage more dialogue. Say:

- I don't blame you for feeling that way.

- Every child your age would feel like that.

- It's okay. I'm here and you are safe.

- It can be hard to talk about it. Let's talk a little more then we can stop if you'd like. We can talk again soon.

- I usually feel better after talking about what's bothering me. Do you feel better yet?

- Not talking is okay once in a while. But never talking about it is a bad idea. You'll just feel worse.
- I'm so glad you talked with me about this. We can talk again any time you want.

Young children may feel responsible for what happened, or feel guilty, even though they have nothing to feel guilty about. It is best to bring this up and reassure the child that he or she was not responsible. Reassurance won't make children feel less guilty right away, but lack of reassurance will prolong their guilt.

- You seem to be saying it was your fault in some way. I know it was not your fault. Please tell me why you think it is?
- Just because you were mad at Mommy yesterday, doesn't mean that you caused her to get sick (have an accident). Sickness and accidents happen. It was not your fault. I know that and Mommy knows that. And we both love you.

An older child may feel guilty about a past disobedient act or angry thoughts about a parent. If that parent has now died or is severely injured, the child may feel like he or she is bad, evil, or unworthy.

- It's normal to be mad at parents. Every kid gets mad and every kid disobeys. Parents expect it—we even did it ourselves when we were younger. But we know that you love us and we always love you no matter how you act.
- Many people feel guilty after someone close to them dies. What I know for sure is that you were loved no matter what.
- I wish I had done some things differently when he was alive. But I know I'm not bad for not having done them. And I know I was deeply loved.
- When someone loves you as much as you were loved, it doesn't matter what you did or didn't do. You were loved no matter what.

Bedwetting/Thumb Sucking/Night Fears

It is essential that parents and caretakers view these regressive behaviors as signs of distress, not as annoying, "childish" behaviors. It is perfectly appropriate to pamper these children for a short time—let them sleep in your bed, let them cuddle with a favorite toy or blanket they had previously given up, let them "cling" to you temporarily. Many children will begin to feel less afraid over many days and naturally resume more age-appropriate behaviors. Others will have to be gently coaxed back into their bed.

Children who wet the bed after having had at least six months of continence are typically more stressed than non-bedwetters. These children also tended to take longer to achieve dry nights.

- The bed is wet? No problem. We can change these sheets in no time.
- It's not unusual for kids your age to wet the bed once in a while, especially if they are worried about something.
- Nightmares can be scary even for grown-ups. I'll stay with you for a while and in a few minutes you'll start to feel better.
- Instead of you sleeping with me tonight, I'll lie down with you in your bed until you feel better and are ready to go back to sleep.

> **If the child says:**
> *But I'm scared!*
> *I'll be afraid if you go back to your bed!*
> *Can't you just stay in bed with me?*
>
> **You reply:**
> *I know you are scared. Nightmares make everybody afraid but the scary feelings don't last. How scared do you feel right now? This much?* (Spread your arms apart to indicate a large space.) *Let's see how long it takes for you to feel only this much afraid.* (Spread your arms apart to indicate a smaller space.)
>
> *Okay. After a few minutes I'll get out of your bed and sit on the floor over here. Maybe later, or tomorrow night, I'll sit just outside your door but it will be open and you'll be able to see me.* (This approach takes time but it gently allows your child to learn to manage feelings by him- or herself.)
>
> *I can stay with you for a while tonight and maybe I'll do that for a few days. But eventually we all need to sleep in our own beds. But I'm never far from you. You've slept alone before and I know you'll feel comfortable again soon.*

- Stop sucking your thumb. I thought you were a big boy?
- Only babies do that.

- *You* wet the bed so you change the sheets. (It's okay to let the child help you change the sheets. But never scold or shame the child.)
- I told you to go back to bed. If you wake me up again you'll be in trouble.
- I hardly slept at all last night because of you.

Disruptive Acting Out

Traumatized or very insecure children may act out with disruptive, mischievous, defiant, or even violent behaviors. If they tended to be more active or difficult to manage before an upsetting event, their behaviors may worsen. Children are not as adept as adults at using thoughts to put things into perspective. They often reveal their emotional state by their actions. Why do some children become aggressive after trauma? Some kids may be reenacting a violent event. Trauma or loss makes people feel helpless and out of control. Aggressive behavior gives people an illusion of control or influence.

After some upsetting event, never view a child's acting out as willful disobedience. It might be wise to ignore some behaviors (temporarily) that are not harmful or too disruptive.

Gently but firmly teach the child what are acceptable and unacceptable behaviors, set clear limits, and be consistent. Spend more time with your child.

- Let's go outside and play hide and seek (throw the ball around, go for a walk, and so on). You guys have a lot of energy to spend.
- I know you've had a rough day but I won't let you speak to me in that tone. Please rephrase it this way. . . .
- I'm sure it bothers you that _____. But I can't allow you to _____.
- You're getting too rough. You'll need to sit down for a while and do _____ instead. Here, I'll do it with you.

Teach your child how to *report* his feelings (usually hurt and anger) instead of acting them out. Teach your child to make requests when he or she is troubled by something rather than to simply be disruptive.

- Sometimes when children feel angry or hurt they act in ways they shouldn't. Maybe they yell at their parents or hit their brothers or refuse to obey. A neat way to handle it differently is to *tell* someone how you are feeling and what you want to happen instead of acting in ways that get you in trouble.

- Tell me "Mom, I'm angry" and I'll listen to what you have to say. If you just scream I'll get upset and won't always listen to what you have to say.

- Let's practice (a very good idea!). Let's pretend you are upset about _____. Now practice telling me how you feel and what you want to happen.

- It's okay to feel mad (sad, nervous, and so on). You can talk about that feeling instead of misbehaving.

- Are there times you remember when you felt mad or sad but did not misbehave or hit your brother? What helped you to control your behavior?

- When you feel like throwing things, what else could you say and do that would help you not get into trouble? Good!

If your child is obstinate and says things like:
No! I won't stop!
I hate you!
You can't tell me what to do!

Keep in mind that he or she is suffering through some loss or trauma. The obstinacy won't last. For a younger child, just make sure he or she doesn't do anything that will cause harm and show that you are approachable. For older children, try to probe for the hurt behind the anger rather than turn this into a power struggle. Your child knows—and you know—that you have the ultimate power.

Cut him some slack and say:
I can't make you stop. At least I can't every time. And I don't blame you for being upset (angry, scared, worried). I won't stand by while you hurt others. But if you want to talk, I'll be here. If you want some time by yourself, I'll still be here later. I love you.

Many kids say that kind of thing under these circumstances. I'll be glad when you realize that you feel differently. You probably don't want to talk about it. But when you do, I promise I'll listen.

It probably seems to you that your life is out of control and that you have little power over what happens. All of us are worried and upset now. If you want to talk about how we can get along better, I'll listen. It's your choice how you want to act. But you understand that there are some things I can't let you do.

How Not to Say It

Avoid vague comments that do not give a child a very clear understanding of what you want. Remember, you want your child to think before he or she acts out. You also need to think and not respond with impulsive reprimands.

- I don't like it when you do that. (*Better:* Stop teasing your sister right now.)
- It would mean a lot to me if you would settle down. (Too wimpy. *Better:* You have to settle down right now. Come with me over here and I'll read to you.)
- We don't do that in this house. (Evidently your child does. Better to simply tell your child to stop and suggest some alternative. Physically guide your child to some other activity if need be.)
- Will you cut that out? (Better to take the child by the hand, tell him what he did that you didn't like, and offer an alternative activity.)
- Why are you being so bad? Can't you see I'm upset? (*Better:* You're hurt and angry. I am too. I can't allow you to act this way. But I'm more than willing to talk. I love you and don't want us to be upset with each other.)

School Refusal

After a loss or trauma, a child may be upset at the thought of returning to school. He may complain about headaches or stomachaches (and they may be real) as a way to forestall having to return. While there can be numerous reasons including academic fears, fear of being bullied, or an inability to make friends, separation anxiety is the main culprit after a loss or trauma. The child is simply afraid to be out of a parent's sight for fear of something bad happening. If parents give in to school refusal the problem just gets worse. After frequent days away from school a child no longer fits in. He is behind in school work and more anxious about being there. Physical symptoms such as stomachache, nausea, or diarrhea will persist if the child is allowed to stay home for these reasons, when the underlying problem is anxiety.

Ultimately, the child needs to learn that whatever fears he has, will not become reality. The only way to realize that is by attending school even when anxiety is high. Parents may be reluctant to force a child to do this, especially if the child has experienced some loss or trauma. But they must. It is okay to allow the child back to school in stages over the course of a week or so. Cooperation with school officials is essential.

Help the child clarify what his or her fears are. Show empathy when appropriate. Be willing to nevertheless take a firm stance.

- When you imagine leaving for school on the bus, what worries you about that?

- What do you fear might happen when you are at school and I am at home (at work)?

- What kinds of things could happen when you are at school that would help you to feel less worried?

- It's normal for kids to have fears like that after what happened.

- Many kids feel the way you do. But your fears are just uncomfortable feelings, they aren't really going to happen.

- I think I would probably want to stay home, too. But I also know that the things you fear won't happen. And you do have to go back to school.

- If you want, you can go to school for just part of the day at first. Would you like to come home after recess or would you like to be dropped off at school in the middle of the day?

- Today I'll be dropping you off at school. The principal knows you'll be coming in late and that's okay. But no matter how upset you get you will still have to stay in school.

- Tomorrow you will stay in school for three classes. The day after you will stay in school for four classes. By the end of the week you'll be staying in all day.

- If you get a stomachache in school or you feel sick, the nurse will check you over. Unless you are very sick you will have to go back to class. If necessary, I'll take you to see the doctor after school.

- I feel bad for you because I know you really would rather stay home. But I know you'll eventually feel no more fear and you'll be happier being with your friends at school.

- Tough. You're going. (Yes, you need to be firm. But you can also be gentle and try to show some empathy. It's bad enough for your child to have to return to school. Don't add salt to the wound by being harsh.)

- But don't you think you'll miss your friends? Don't you think you'd rather be able to play at recess instead of stay home here? (It's unlikely your child will be persuaded. Better to simply state that when he returns to school one of the benefits will be being with friends. Don't debate that. Just say it.)

- I'd really like it if you went to school. (This effort at being gentle is too wimpy. Simply say that he or she will go to school. Be gentle by showing some empathy. *Better:* You will be going to school in an hour. I know you don't want to and I wish you felt better. But I know it's best for you to go.)

- You can't go if you feel sick. (Don't give in.)

- All right. You can stay home another few days but then you really have to go to school. (You're caving in. Get your child to school as quickly as possible. It only gets harder for each of you the longer it takes to return to school.)

It's hard to be patient and understanding with the children when I am stressed out, too. Any tips?

So often, tragedy or trauma affects an entire family, not just one individual. Parents aren't superhuman and will undoubtedly mishandle some situations with their kids during trying times. If you are a single parent your job is doubly difficult. In addition to the more obvious suggestions such as making sure you have friends to talk to and lean on, examine your inner dialogue. Chances are you are making some wrong assumptions that are adversely affecting your ability to cope. For example, when kids are experiencing a loss or trauma and are showing symptoms, you might blame yourself for being ineffective. You may then get angry with the kids because they've become the mirrors that reflect your inability to bring peace or soothe their feelings. Better to remind yourself that you need not be perfect, that you are capable (although preoccupied and stressed out yourself), that the bad times are temporary, and that spending time with the kids and offering reassurances can go a long way toward healing.

How to Listen Ten Times Better

The insanity of this is becoming scary, and it's all happening so fast.

—Steve D., eighth grader, on 9/11 terrorist attacks

The school shooting happened a hundred miles away from Samantha's school but it received national attention. Within days, schools in the state were not only practicing fire drills but also "lock-in" drills. Children were taught how to crouch under their desks or stand with backs against the walls in case the school had a dangerous intruder. Or in case bullets were flying.

Samantha accepted all these new procedures without apparent anxiety. Some of the kids in her class found the safety exercises to be exciting and adventurous, although they made her best friend feel scared. Samantha spoke of all this during dinner one evening.

"They make us line up against the walls in the classroom. It wasn't like a fire drill where we had to go outside. It made Jennifer nervous."

Her father said, "But there's nothing to be nervous about, right? They are just teaching you a better way to be safe."

Her mother said, "It was awful what happened at that other school. Were you nervous, too?"

"Maybe a little," Samantha answered.

"You'll be fine," Mom said. "Shootings are very rare. After a while you won't even think about it."

"And you can talk to us about this any time you want," Dad said.

Samantha nodded her head and resumed eating.

Were Samantha's concerns really dealt with? Do you think she felt better after this conversation? Is she more or less likely to bring up the subject again? If you were to ask the parents if they listened well, they would claim they did. They didn't ignore their daughter's comments, they responded to her use of the word "nervous" and they both tried to reassure her that she was safe. Her dad even invited her to bring up the topic again. But their effort missed the mark.

Parents often react to a child's fears and worries like they would to an injured finger: they act to bring relief. For a cut finger it's a simple matter of antibiotic cream and a Band-Aid, and perhaps a kiss to make it all better. But that approach falls short when it comes to emotional injuries. In their need to make it all better, parents often don't listen well although they'd swear an oath that they do.

Had Samantha's mom and dad been patient listeners they would not have jumped in to console her without first making sure they knew what was really on her mind. If a child has unspoken fears but a parent says there is nothing to be afraid about, the child may feel that talking about them will be a waste of time. Or, she may feel that there must be something wrong with her to feel the way she does. In either case, open conversation is shut off, even though the parents meant well.

With just a few changes, Samantha's folks might have listened better and the conversation might have gone like this:

Samantha: "They make us line up against the walls in the classroom. It wasn't like a fire drill where we had to go outside. It made Jennifer nervous."

Dad: "So fire drills are okay but these new drills make some kids nervous." (He briefly summarizes his understanding of what Samantha said. It shows he was listening and makes Samantha feel understood.)

S: "Yeah. It's like the teachers are telling us that shootings can happen here and we have to be ready."

M: "Is that what everyone is thinking? That a shooting can happen at your school?" (Instead of rushing in to reassure her, Mom asks her daughter to elaborate. That gives Samantha another opportunity to express herself.)

S: "Yeah. Could it happen?"

M: "It's normal for everyone to worry about that. (Mom picks up on the fact that Samantha is nervous, even though she never admitted it.) But the truth is that shootings are very rare."

D: "And now all the schools are taking steps to prevent future shootings, so they will be even less likely to happen."

M: "What do you think about that?" (Mom has paid close enough attention to realize that Samantha is concerned and wants to find out if Dad's reassurance helped.)

S: "It makes me feel a little better."

M: "I wonder what you'd like to hear or see happen that would make you feel even better than that?" (Mom heard the words *a little better* and understood them to mean that Samantha still felt uneasy.)

And so on.

Their conversation has continued with more helpful information because Mom and Dad were willing to listen patiently. One clue to effective listening is that conversations tend to run longer because a good listener prompts the speaker to elaborate and clarify what's being said. Poor listening cuts off communication quickly.

Parents need improvement in the listening department if they

- instinctively try to fix a child's upset feelings before fully understanding them.
- tend to be perfectionistic and have a strong need to be right. Perfectionistic parents convey disapproval more than encouragement and children may avoid bringing up fears or worries in anticipation of being told they are wrong for feeling that way.
- tend to be irritable and cranky much of the time. They will not have the patience required to listen.
- are overprotective. Overprotective parents see their kids as emotional extensions of themselves and presume that they really know their children's needs when in fact they sometimes confuse their kids' needs with their own. They therefore stop listening because they do not want to hear anything that would contradict their perspective.
- are unhappy with their partner. They may then unwittingly use a child as a way to express dissatisfaction with their partner. They may overindulge a child or be overly strict—not because they have truly listened to their children and understand what is needed—but because they want to make a political point.
- are too busy in life. Instead, they will have "drive through conversations" that attempt to get quickly to the "bottom line." However, children and adults often need to take their time while talking in order to bring out all that they are feeling.
- become uncomfortable with strong emotions.
- are overwhelmed or preoccupied with their own problems.

- believe that children are oblivious or unconcerned about problems going on around them.
- regard chitchats as unimportant conversations. In fact, chitchats can lead to important topics and may contain clues to underlying concerns. If a child enjoys regular chitchat with a parent, he or she is more likely to discuss problems when they come up.

You won't "Say It" well if you don't listen well. There are just a few simple guidelines to help you improve your listening skills. Follow them and you will learn much more about your child's view of the world.

Don't assume when your child tells you something that he or she has given you the whole story. Ask for more information, then sit back, and listen. (The "S" in SAFE stands for search.)

- Tell me more about that.
- That's interesting. I'd like to hear more.
- What else happened?
- Any other feelings you have about that?
- Are there other things about this topic that you think about but don't necessarily talk about?

If the child can't elaborate, say:

- It isn't always easy to explain. (That shows that you have, in fact, *listened* to the child's inability to elaborate.)
- Sometimes we all have a hard time explaining why we feel the way we do.
- That's okay. What else can you tell me?
- That's okay. I'll ask later on. Maybe you'll have something to add then.
- You did a great job so far. Maybe there isn't anything else for you to add. Maybe there is.
- If you were talking about this with your best friend (imaginary friend, teacher, favorite aunt, and so on) is there anything else you might say?

Briefly summarize your understanding of what you heard without judging, lecturing, or advising.

- You're telling me that you are sad about what happened.

- You feel scared at night when the lights are out. Do I have that right?
- You worry that something bad might happen to you or Mommy or Daddy.
- You are worried that the tornado will happen again.
- It scares you to think that Daddy could get hurt or killed when he is at work.
- You worry every time I go to the mailbox that there will be anthrax.
- You're afraid that if I get sick I will die, too, just like Grandma did.

Pay attention to your child's use of strong words or emotionally laden words. Pay attention if your child's reaction is inappropriate or overdone (such as when he easily gets angry over a small thing). Pay attention if your child is getting defensive.

- You said that what you saw on TV made you *worried*. Tell me more.
- When I asked if you wanted to come with me to the mall you said "No." But you said it like something was on your mind. What's on your mind?
- You said that your friend was very sad. I wonder how that made you feel?
- I just saw you fold your arms and walk away mad. I wonder if I did something that you didn't like?
- You seem so *relieved.*
- It's wonderful to see you so much *happier* today.
- You just snapped at me. You don't usually do that so something must be on your mind. I'd really like to hear what it is. (Older kids and teenagers can get disrespectful and have a bad attitude. If there has been a recent loss or trauma, don't make their disrespect the key issue—you'll miss the opportunity to understand what's really bothering them.)
- The way you just sighed makes me think you are upset about something. Talk to me about it and I promise I'll listen.

If the child—or particularly the teenager—is complaining, defensive, critical, or otherwise hard to listen to, find something you can agree with before you show anger or hostility or before you tell him why he is wrong to feel the way he does. Admit to any of your own mistakes. Try not to get defensive.

- You've said a lot just now. You're right about . . .
- I see your point about . . .
- That makes sense.
- I see why you might feel that way.

- I would feel the same way if I were you.
- You're right. I should not have said . . .

If you are finding it hard to listen because your child is too upset or disruptive or rude, say:

- I hear you. Can we sit down over here and continue the conversation.
- I want to listen better but it's hard for me when you raise your voice. Please speak more quietly.
- I see you are really upset. I can't listen to you very well if I am worried about what you might do next. Let's sit down and talk.
- I'll be fair to you and listen. But then you need to be fair to me and hear me out.

How Not to Say It

- You don't really think that, do you?
- Yes, but . . . (Don't challenge beliefs without first showing that you understand them or that the child's feelings make sense.)
- Didn't we talk about this before? (If it's being repeated, chances are it is important to your child and unresolved. Listen to that unstated message.)
- Hurry up. (Show that you are willing to take the time to listen.)
- Fine, but can you get to the point? (If your child seems to be wandering aimlessly in conversation or getting sidetracked with unimportant details, put him on track by saying, *The main thing you seem to be saying is . . . Can you tell me more about . . . Is the most important thing you want me to understand so far the fact that . . .*)
- Okay, okay. Can I talk now? (You are showing impatience, not interest.)
- Don't worry about it. (This phrase is fine but the timing is important. Said too soon it will choke off further discussion and you may be left with an inadequate understanding of your child's worries.)
- Why won't you talk to me? I want to listen! (Actually, you are not listening to the fact that your child does not want to talk. Connect without being disagreeable. *Better:* I can see you'd rather not talk right now. I hope you change your mind. I think it's important that we talk. I always appreciate it when we do talk.)
- I refuse to listen to you if you're going to act that way. (In normal, non-traumatic situations, this may be helpful. But if your child has been troubled by recent events, *listen* to the way he is acting—that is, take the behavior

as a cue to how he is feeling and comment on that. *Better:* I don't blame you for being so upset. But I find that I can't listen very well unless we're both a little calmer.)

What is the main problem parents have with listening effectively to their children?

The main problem is that parents think they are already (reasonably) effective listeners so they don't try to improve their skill. (Telling a parent he could be a better listener is like saying he could be a better driver. He's had years of experience and will conclude he is capable enough.) Parents of infants must learn to listen in order to respond to their babies needs. Parents of toddlers listen, too, but a toddler's needs are fairly simple. Parents have an intuitive understanding of many concerns a young child might have so they stop listening and focus on solving the problem. That's all well and good until the child is older and capable of more introspection. Unfortunately, parents still presume they fully understand what's going on in the child's mind when in fact the child is developing more complex wants and needs.

Listening to a child is never more important than during scary or sad times. Parents should not overlook any improvements they need in the listening department. Their kids will be better off for it.

9

How to Express Your Emotions Without Overwhelming Your Child

I have a dream that there would be no such word as **violence** *or* **terrorism** *. . . that everybody would be able to go to school and laugh . . . that my parents wouldn't be so overprotective over a chance of another terrorism act.*

—Rachel L., age 14

Adults may know that "it's okay to cry" but many feel uneasy shedding tears in front of children. They do not want to alarm their kids or appear weak and vulnerable. Despair, intense grief, loneliness, shock, and anger—these are common emotions during times of trauma, fear, or loss—yet parents often wish to shield their children from these emotional displays.

Can a parent's emotional response to trauma overwhelm a child? Yes. But hiding feelings or pretending that all is fine is not a solution to that concern. Besides, some intense emotional reactions cannot be helped. When American Airlines flight 587 nosedived into a residential section of Queens, New York in November 2001, the fear and horror residents experienced could not be tucked away. Even expected losses such as the death of a loved one who has been ill can trigger intense emotional reactions.

A parent or other adult who loses emotional control can frighten a child. But the child will probably handle it under various conditions:

- If another parent or caretaker possesses more emotional control and is able to comfort the child;

- If the parent who is very emotional is able to recover and show that despite being very grieved or upset, he or she will be okay and can resume parenting duties;

- If the parent can convey the attitude that despite tremendous upset, the family will recover (somehow);

- If the parent is eventually able to reassure the child that life is more bearable despite the pain of loss;

- If the child has good friends and many interests.

If you display intense sadness and grief, talk to your child as soon as you have regained some degree of control and offer reassurances. Say things like:

- I'll be fine. I am just very, very sad right now.

- I'm feeling better than I was a little while ago. But I'll probably have some moments when I am feeling very sad again.

- You must have felt worried when you saw me so upset. I'm sorry if I scared you. I'll be okay. I'm just sad.

- What were you thinking when you saw me so upset?

- It can be scary for kids to see their parents so upset. But you don't have to be afraid of anything. I'm okay, just very sad.

    Strong feelings of anger are not unusual during grief, especially if the trauma was horrific and unjust. However, children and teens will be more frightened by your intense anger than by your sadness. If you express rage, find a way to comfort your child as soon as possible.

- I'm angry about what happened but I shouldn't have been so angry in front of you. I'm sure it scared you. I'll be more careful next time I feel that angry.

- I have a right to be angry but I shouldn't have scared you the way I did. (Show affection.)

- I'm sorry for making you upset.

- I didn't want to scare you. Let's sit down together for a while.

- Yes, I'm angry, but underneath my anger is sadness. I am very sad over what happened. How do you feel?

It is helpful when expressing strong emotions to remain seated. Also, try to keep your voice in the range of normal conversational volume. Both of these tips will help you feel more in control.

Display intense anger only when your kids are not around. When they are near, *report* your anger but do not display it by shouting, flailing your arms, punching walls, and so on.

- It was wrong for those people to kill other innocent people. I am very angry.

- I am furious about what happened.

- I am angry because what happened to us was wrong and unfair.

- Some days I'm not quite as angry as I am now. I know that eventually I will feel less angry. But it might take a long time.

Children need to know that no matter how you are feeling you are in charge and can be counted on. They need to feel secure. This can be difficult for you in the aftermath of some trauma. Normal activities such as preparing breakfast may seem surreal. At best you may be only able to "go through the motions." But going through the motions is fine.

Even if your emotions are running high, find time to provide structure to your children's lives. It shows that things can be somewhat normal and that you haven't lost control.

- I want to go over your homework with you later.

- I can't go over your homework with you now. I want to but I'm too upset. Let's plan on doing some of it tomorrow.

- Please set the table for dinner.

- Turn the TV off in five minutes. It's time for bed.

- I'm going to rake some leaves. Would you help me bag them when I'm finished?

- Let's go see a movie today. It will help take our mind off of what's happened.

- I don't have the energy to prepare dinner. How about we get some fast food?

- I haven't felt much like cleaning up this house lately. I'm doing what I can for now. I'll feel better soon.

Show thanks and appreciation for efforts your child is making to be helpful. It not only makes your child feel better, it will help you to feel more in control of your emotions.

- You've been so helpful to me today. Thank you so much. I know it hasn't been easy for you these days.
- It was so helpful to me when you unloaded the dishwasher.
- You didn't argue with your brother when he insisted on watching a different TV program. Thanks for doing that.
- I love you.

Don't be indifferent to the impact your reaction is having on your kids. Don't act as if your kids are expected to put aside their needs and take care of your needs.

- My life is over.
- I'll never be happy again.
- I wish I were dead.
- Get away from me! Leave me alone! (*Better:* I need some time to be alone right now. If I can help you quickly I will. Otherwise, it will have to wait.)
- Get it yourself! Can't you see I'm upset?
- Nothing matters to me anymore. (Your child will think that he/she no longer matters.)

After some disaster, loss, or frightening experience, it is normal to feel somewhat overprotective of your children. Don't become obsessed. Don't say things like:

- I will never let you out of my sight.
- The world is very dangerous. You can never feel perfectly safe unless I am with you.
- You can't trust anybody. (Children need people to trust in order to feel secure.)
- You can never go to a mall (a friend's house, a movie, and so on) unless I am with you.
- You don't really want to sleep over at your friend's house, do you? You know I worry about you when you're not here.

Please explain how a child might be overwhelmed by a parent's emotional outburst during scary times. What else can parents do to make sure that their emotional reactions won't become part of the problem?

Whether children experience a frightening disaster personally or even observe it on TV, they can immediately feel insecure about their world. Beliefs they had such as "The world is a reasonable safe place . . . Children will grow up to become adults . . . My life is predictable . . ." have been shattered. After the 9/11 attack, many children who heard planes overhead days later feared for their lives. Kids who witness shootings can jump at the sound of a loud bang. Children who lived through a devastating hurricane or tornado can be frightened by any storm. And if these children watch their parents scream or cry uncontrollably, they can feel afraid and insecure unless the parent is able to reassure them that all will be okay despite strong feelings.

When parents are very upset and traumatized by some event, I recommend they spend quiet time every day with their kids. If the child is young enough, hold him or her in a chair and rock, or read stories, or sing favorite songs. Don't do this only for a few minutes but for as long as possible. Spend time with a teenager doing something together—go for a walk, play a video game, watch a ballgame, go shopping. Connect every day to your children. You need to be both physically present and psychologically present.

How to Encourage a Reluctant Child to Talk

10

I hold feelings inside. Like right now I'm trying not to cry.

—Antwan J., age 14

After his grandfather died, Billy withdrew. Occasionally he'd mention how he missed his grandfather but most of the time he kept his feelings to himself. Billy had been very close to his grandfather. They'd spent a lot of time together since they lived near each other. It was unusual for Billy to be so quiet and withdrawn. His parents tried to get him to talk about how he felt but were not very successful.

After trauma, loss, or upsetting events it is important to talk about how you feel. You don't have to gush with emotion or speak about every detail. And while you are entitled to keep thoughts to yourself, it is to your advantage to speak up. Why? Research is clear that opening up sparks a healing process that is impeded when you don't open up. Children, including teenagers, especially need to talk because they don't have the wisdom and life experience to put tragedy into any meaningful perspective. (In fact, adults don't usually know what to make of senseless tragedies.) Without a dialogue, people of all ages can feel more alone and more helpless.

Things to consider:

- A usually talkative child may still be reluctant to express thoughts and feelings after a severe loss or trauma. Children who have been abused, for example, often feel guilty and bad and therefore are afraid to open up for fear of being blamed. Parents need to give these children time and reassure them they will not be blamed.

- Some kids are especially sensitive to ongoing marital and family problems and may not wish to add to a family's burden by revealing their personal fears or worries. Parents must get across the message that no matter what the child reveals they will not be devastated or unable to function.

- Older kids who have been taught to routinely put aside their needs for the sake of younger kids ("Oh, Mary, let your little brother sit there. You're older and should be more mature") may have a hard time justifying their right to express difficult emotions.

- Kids who are typically more closemouthed to begin with should be encouraged to draw, play act, or write out their feelings.

Acknowledge your child's reluctance to talk. Encourage dialogue without getting pushy or annoyed.

- A lot of kids have a hard time talking about their feelings after going through what you went through. But they usually feel better after they talk about it.

- I don't blame you for being quiet about it. It can be hard to talk about it. But I really do want to listen.

- Okay, I can see you don't want to talk now. I'll keep asking you from time to time because I know you'll feel better if you can talk about your feelings.

Older kids may have insight into why they'd rather not talk. Inquire.

- What could happen that would make it easier for you to talk?

- If your best friend asked you why you don't like to talk about it, what would your answer be?

- I noticed that sometimes you do open up a little. What is different about those times? What happens then that makes it okay for you to talk?

- If you and I were to talk, would there be something you would not want me to ask about?

- Is it easier for you to talk with me or with Mom (Dad, Grandma, and so on)?

- How about we just talk for five minutes. When the time is up we can stop, unless you decide you want to continue.

For nontalkative children age eight and under, have available four drawings: a happy face, a sad face, a scared face, and a neutral face. Use these to help identify your child's feelings.

- Okay, you don't have to talk now if you don't want to. How about pointing to these pictures instead? When _____ happened, which face best shows how you felt?

- This is the happy face. What has happened since _____ that has made you feel happy?

- Which of these faces describes how you feel most of the time?

- When you are playing, which face shows how you usually feel? When you are lying in bed before you fall asleep, which face shows how you feel? When you are home with the family, which face shows how you feel?

Tell your child how you think he/she might be feeling. Use behavior as clues.

- When you sit very quietly like that I think you might be feeling sad.

- When you yell and get mad about little things, it makes me think you are really upset about something else. Something like _____.

- I am feeling sad and a little scared over what happened. I'm guessing you feel that way, too. But I know things will work out. I'm not sure you think that, however.

- If I were you, I'd be feeling _____ right now.

- Sometimes I think you want to talk and you don't want to talk at the same time.

- Most kids worry if _____ will ever happen again. I think you might be worrying about that, too.

- You might be feeling very angry about what happened. That's normal.

- Sometimes I think you want be to be quiet and not have me ask you how you are feeling. Sometimes I think you want me to ask.

Praise any effort by your child to open up.

- I'm so glad you said that.

- I'm proud of you for having the courage to tell me that.

- I feel better now that you told me how you feel. I hope you feel better, too.

- You told me a little of what's on your mind. That's great. Maybe you'll decide to tell me more later.

Don't criticize your child for not speaking up. Don't ignore the small openings he/she might give you for a dialogue (usually at inopportune times). Don't take the attitude that your child will speak up when he's ready—he may not speak up at all.

- How do you expect me to help you if you won't cooperate?

- You're just being stubborn. (That is not likely. If your child is distressed, he has reasons for not opening up. They may be irrational reasons but they are real to your child.)

- Finally, you started to tell me something! It's about time! Why couldn't you have told me before? (Don't make your child wrong. Welcome the conversation.)

- I'd like to hear more but it's getting late (I'm too busy . . . I'm too tired . . . I don't have time. . . .). Make time. A child who is already reluctant to talk may not give you another chance.

- Oh my God! You poor baby! You had a horrible experience! It must have frightened you to death! (A little less drama. Also, don't talk so much. Give your child room to express him- or herself without you interrupting so soon. Put your arm around your child and focus on listening more than speaking.)

How can I tell the difference between a child who needs to talk but won't, and a child who says little because he/she is not really all that upset?

If your child was usually talkative before some upsetting loss or event and is now not speaking up, odds are that he or she is holding back. If your child was involved personally in some major upsetting event or knows somebody who was involved, that child probably needs to talk even if he or she seems untroubled. One couple never discussed the World Trade Center bombing with their five-year-old daughter. She never brought it up either and the couple assumed she was unaware. Yet when the father announced he was going on a business trip to New York City the girl became hysterical, believing her father would die if he went there. That child showed no signs of worry prior to that, but clearly she was troubled by the events of the world.

If your child witness some horror on TV, don't assume it didn't register. You're better off raising the topic and finding out how your child feels and thinks.

If your child is displaying any behavioral problems, withdrawal, regressive symptoms such as bedwetting or extra clinging, a decline in grades, irritability, or any other change in mood after some major world or local calamity, talking is essential. A child who is unaffected by scary events will act happy and normal.

Finally, examine your own level of reluctance to talk with your child about what's happening in the world. The more reluctant you are, the more you may convince yourself that your child is just fine and you may overlook signs and symptoms that contradict your perspective.

Special Case: What to Say When a Loved One Is Killed

11

Dear Dad,
I will never leave you. Right now I am scared about Papa, but at least we love
each other. I love you and our family so much that my heart is big. I don't care
about presents. All I care about is our family.

—Kyle S., age 9, in a letter to his father after the unexpected death of his beloved grandfather

It is hard to explain death and loss to kids. They don't really understand why someone they know and love has to leave so soon (does anybody?). Very young children don't comprehend the finality of death. In a manner that is touching and heartbreaking, they still look for their loved one when they open the door to their homes. They sit on Dad's chair, on their sister's bed, on their best friend's front porch and wait for them to return, to say "Here I am. I'm back!"

Older children know that death is final. Yet, many still pray that it was all a bad dream.

Surviving adults know that loved ones killed in some senseless act of devastation won't return. It is their job to explain that to the kids in a manner they can understand. It's their job to provide comfort.

When the world becomes a scary place and a loved one is killed by some act of violence, force of nature, or even by accident, keep these points in mind when talking to kids:

- Younger children may repeatedly ask when the loved one will return. Even if you explain that the person is not coming back, don't be surprised to hear such responses as, *"But will he be here for my birthday party?"*

- If the death was violent or witnessed, children may experience nightmares. These can continue for weeks or months. If the nightmares are disruptive or the child shows other signs of traumatic stress, consult an experienced professional.

- Children grieve in waves. They may be crying one minute and playing ball the next. Don't mistake a child's playing as a sign that he or she is "over it." It's always a good idea to talk periodically about the loved one who has died.

- Holidays and anniversaries are especially difficult for many people. Try to acknowledge the absent family member with some brief ritual such as a prayer or by browsing through photographs. Don't avoid bringing up the person's memory. It will be on everyone's mind.

- If a loved one's death brought national attention as did victims from the Oklahoma City bombing, the 9/11 attack, or a major storm, children may be subjected to repetitive television images and perhaps inquiries from the media. Limit TV viewing. Feel free to say no to media requests that make you uncomfortable.

- Omit graphic and grisly details of a person's death.

- There are numerous books for children to help them deal with death and dying. One fiction story by this author is *Where the Balloons Go*, suitable for kids age eight and under. The Centering Corporation, a nonprofit organization with an extensive list of books and tapes, publishes it. The Centering Corporation often donates thousands of dollars worth of books to areas hit by devastation. For a catalog call 402-553-1200.

Be direct but sensitive when giving the news. Make sure you touch or hold the child. Let your words and actions convey that you are ready to discuss the matter and that you wish to offer comfort.

- I have some sad news. There was a shooting and . . .

- Your dad was on the plane that crashed. Daddy died. He's in heaven with God now and he won't be coming back.

- People in our neighborhood were killed today by a bad man with a gun. Everybody is very sad and shocked.

- Your friend's house caught fire last night. I'm so sorry but your friend died.
- Your mom died trying to save another person's life. She is a hero and we all miss her so much.

Don't stifle any emotional reaction your child may have.

- It's okay to cry.
- I'm sad, too.
- Just let it out.
- Let me hold you.
- This is hard for you. It's hard for all of us.

Children may feel guilt for not having treated the deceased person well recently. They may feel responsible for the death. You won't be able to change these notions immediately but you need to be alert for them.

- Yes, Grandpa was driving you to school when he had the accident and died. But it was not your fault. It was an accident and no one was at fault (or, it was the fault of the other driver, the wet road, and so on). Grandpa wanted to be with you. He died doing what he wanted to do.
- I can understand why you feel so bad because you argued with your brother just yesterday. You wish you had been nicer to him. But just as you know you love him even though you argued, he loved you, too. And he knows you loved him. Brothers don't always get along. Every brother fights once in while. Maybe soon you'll realize that you have nothing to feel guilty about.
- Even though you feel guilt for what happened, I know you are not guilty and I do not blame you.
- You feel bad that the teacher died and you had made fun of that teacher. Kids don't always say wonderful things about their teachers and all teachers realize that. Your teacher was once a child and she probably said some bad things about her teachers. If it would make you feel better, you can write a letter to her family and tell them the good things about her.

Explain the concept of death to younger children. According to grief expert Dr. David Crenshaw, young children need to be told that the body completely stops working after death.

- When we die our body stops working. We don't move, we don't see or hear or taste or smell anything. Our heart stops beating. We never feel any pain.

- It looks like we are asleep but being dead is not the same as being asleep. After we fall asleep we can wake up. We do not get up and move around after we die.

- Our body no longer feels hot or cold.

Your child may have concerns about his or her (or your) safety. Offer reassurances. Kids under six need a sense of security. This is not the time to tell them that life is uncertain and that safety cannot be assured. Older children who understand that death can happen to anyone still need reassurance that their death or yours are very unlikely.

- (To a young child) I'm fine. I will be with you. I'm not going to die for a long, long time. You will be very old by the time I die.

- Everybody will eventually die. But most people live to be very old. I expect to live to be old and you will live that long, too.

- You seem to be very worried now that I've gotten the flu. I'll be fine. Most sicknesses people get are not dangerous. I'll be all better in a few days.

- Yes, people do die from car accidents. But most people do not die in accidents. I am also a careful driver. I can see why you might worry but there really is no need to.

- It's normal to be afraid to go to school when you heard about a shooting at school. But the school is more protected now. I wouldn't let you go there if I believed you would be in danger.

- It's normal to worry about the people you love after someone has died so suddenly. But over time you will feel less worried and you will trust that things usually work out okay.

- I notice that you don't like to say goodbye in the morning when you go to school. What worries you?

- What could happen that would make you feel safer?

Even young children are capable of attending funerals and wakes. Some may be more frightened than others. Explain ahead of time what to expect. If your child is skittish or does not wish to attend—no matter how old—find some other way for him or her to be part of the ritual for saying good-bye (such as writing a letter or drawing a picture for the deceased).

- At the wake you will see _____'s body in the casket. She probably won't look exactly like she did when she was alive. A person's appearance changes a little after death.

- Many people will be there. They will walk over to the casket one at a time and look at the person. They will probably say a prayer.

- Some people will be crying. Everybody will feel very sad.

- At the funeral, we will all say some prayers. After we leave the casket will be lowered in the ground. The person in the casket does not feel afraid and does not know that it is dark.

- The body was cremated. That means that the body was put under a great light that burns the body. The person never feels any pain. When it is over what's left are called ashes. They look like small pebbles and sand. That is what remains of the person's body.

Explain spiritual matters as you see fit.

- Everybody has a spirit. Our spirit is the most important part of who we are and it lives forever. Your daddy's spirit is alive right now. When it is our turn to die, we will be with each other as spirits.

- While it's nice to know that your brother's spirit is alive, we cannot see him or hold him and that is hard for us. We'd rather have him here with us.

- You can talk to _____ and I believe she will hear you, even though we cannot see or hear her.

- She is in heaven with God. We will all be there one day.

Don't use misleading words or phrases.

- Daddy is asleep forever. (Children may be afraid to go to sleep if you say that.)

- Grandma got sick and died. (Children get sick, too. *Better:* Grandma was very, very sick. She was much sicker than you or I have ever been, and the medicines could not help her, so she died.)

- The people who died are on a long journey. (Kids go on journeys.)

- She went to the hospital and died. (A child might think that going to the hospital was the cause of death.)

Don't give reassurances that are unbelievable.

- I will never die. (It's better to tell a young child that you expect to live a very long time.)

- No one you love is going to die.

- Only old people die.

If your child responds:

But Mommy didn't live long. How do you know that you will?
But what if you and Daddy die. What will happen to me?
Do dogs and cats go to heaven, too?

You say:

All I know is that most people live to be very old. I can't be completely sure that I will live to an old age, but I am as certain as I possibly can be. And I do try to take care of myself and I'm always careful.

That is not likely to happen. It is very unusual for that to happen. If it did happen, you will probably be much older and have a family of your own by then. If it happened when you were still young, you would live with _____ and they would take care of you.

I believe that they do. If we love our pets, I think God would want us to be with them in heaven. I like thinking that.

Don't allow your grief to overwhelm your child.

- I'll never be happy again. (*Better:* I'm very sad now and I can't be happy. But I know that eventually I'll feel less sad and I'll be able to smile when I remember _____.)

- I'll never get over it.

- Go away. I just want to lie down.

My husband and brother were killed in a car accident during a blizzard. When my son returned to school after the funerals, he felt very self-conscious. Some children spoke to him about what happened. Some didn't. He felt everybody was staring at him. On top of that he was grieving over the loss of his dad and uncle. Is there a helpful way to prepare a child to return to school after some tragedy?

Some children appreciate the acknowledgments their classmates offer and some prefer to keep matters low-key. It's usually a good idea to talk with your child before he returns to school and get an idea of what might be best. Knowledge of your child's personality helps, too. A very shy child, for example, may feel more uncomfortable if he or she is singled out in class while the teacher expresses the class's sympathy. Whatever you decide, present your ideas and concerns to the teacher(s) and they can help coordinate some kind of appropriate gesture of condolence. Your son, for example, might appreciate a card signed by all of his classmates. Or, he may not want his teacher to make some public presentation that calls attention to his grief. He may be afraid of crying in front of his classmates. You can ask the teacher to give suggestions to classmates on what they should say (or not say) upon his return. For example, he might not mind hearing someone say, "I'm so sorry that your dad died" but he may be uncomfortable answering questions such as "How did he die?"

Special Case: What to Say When Your Child Has Been Sexually Abused

12

The little girls with the glass eyes can only play with the snow on their window sill....

—Ilse L., age 13, from her poem, *Fear*

According to best estimates, between 12 percent and 25 percent of children will experience some form of sexual abuse. It may be a one-time only incident but most cases of abuse happen more than once over a course of weeks or even years. Children of all ages are at risk but the most vulnerable age is between eight and twelve. Girls are assaulted at about twice the rate of boys.

Sexually abused children often feel ashamed. Many think that they are "bad" or at fault. Psychologist Cynthia Monahon, author of *Children and Trauma: A Guide for Parents and Professionals*, says that 20 percent to 60 percent of sexually abused children may show no behavioral disturbances. The most reliable sign that a child has been abused is age-inappropriate sexual behavior or knowledge. Many children under age twelve will not want to discus feelings of shame. Parents must be willing to go at their child's pace. Problems occur when there is a mismatch between how much a parent needs to discuss what happened and how much a child needs to talk.

Parents must be prepared to talk about the abuse and its impact many times, probably over the course of years. They need to convey that the child was not bad, or to blame and that steps have been taken to prevent such a thing from recurring.

Especially reread chapters 6 to 10 in this book for many additional suggestions and insights. This topic is too important to be adequately covered in one chapter.

In the immediate aftermath, you need to show your love and offer a great deal of encouragement. Some abused children may welcome affection, others might tense up. Proceed cautiously and do not overwhelm your child.

- It was not your fault. It doesn't matter that you trusted that person. He was the adult and he was the only one to blame for what happened.
- Unfortunately, what happened to you happens to so many children. None of them are responsible. You are not responsible.
- I love you and will always love you no matter what happens.
- You are feeling awful now but I know that you will feel better over time.
- The person who did this to you will be punished. He will not harm you anymore.
- I will always be available to talk to you about this. Some days you might not want to talk and that is okay. Some days you might want to talk a lot and that is okay, too.
- There is nothing you can tell me about what happened that will make me mad at you.
- It's over now. You're safe.
- We will learn ways to protect you so this will never happen to you again.
- It's normal to feel scared even after some time has gone by. But you will feel better eventually.

It is important that a child talk about what happened to a trusted adult. However, older children may be embarrassed or reluctant to talk about certain details with a parent. Perhaps a teacher, school counselor, or beloved relative would make him- or herself available to talk.

- Tell me what happened. I know it might be difficult to talk about but I know it can help you feel better.
- Sometimes when a child is abused _____ happens. Did that happen to you?
- That must have been so scary for you.
- You're doing fine talking about this.

- What else happened?

- What were you afraid of when it happened? Did you worry about _____?

- Many children worry that they will be blamed for what happened. Did you ever worry about that?

- Were you afraid that something bad would happen if you told an adult what was happening?

- A similar thing happened to me when I was a child . . . (It's okay to discuss your history when relevant. Make sure you offer hope.)

   Weeks and months later, your child might still have fears that are triggered by such things as a television show, a certain sound, or some conversations overheard in school. Be alert and understanding.

- I bet that TV show reminded you of the abuse. I'm sorry you had to see that. Would you like to talk about it?

- Anyone who has been abused will feel scared or mad from time to time, especially when they see something that reminds them of what happened. When was the last time you felt like this?

- I wonder if things happen in school that make you think about the abuse?

- You are brave talking about this. (Be careful. This may indeed help a child feel better. But what if this same child is reluctant to talk in the future? What if he or she is holding back now? The child won't feel brave and that comment may make him or her feel worse.)

- You should have known better.

- Why didn't you say something sooner? (*Better:* You probably thought about saying something sooner but were afraid.)

- This is horrible! This is the worst thing that could ever happen! (Tone down your emotions. Your child needs reassurance that all will be okay.)

- Didn't I tell you never to let anybody touch you there? (This is blaming your child. Never do that.)

- From now on never talk to strangers. (First of all, people known to your child, not strangers, do most sexual abuse. Second, it is unrealistic for a child to never talk to any stranger. What about the cashier? The new teacher? The person sitting next to you at church or in the plane? If your child ever got lost, he or she might need to speak to a stranger and ask for assistance.)

What clues can I look for that my child might have been sexually abused?

Age-inappropriate sexual behavior or knowledge (exposing oneself to other children, having dolls engage in sex, drawing pictures of sexual acts, and so on) are prime clues. Since some sexually abused children display no behavioral signs of trauma, you have to look for indirect clues. Changes in school performance often indicate a problem somewhere in the child's life. Unusual clinging behavior or sudden fears or genital pain may also indicate abuse. Teens who are promiscuous at an early age may have been abused. As a parent, you must try to be aware of any sign that matters are not right and be able to talk to your child about it.

Talking about the possibility of sexual abuse before it happens lets kids know that this is a topic you can talk about.

13

35 Good Answers to 35 Tough Questions

Dear Mr. Bush,
Is this what the world is coming to—that we need acts of terrorism to show us
that lives are important? Shouldn't we have hung our flags all the days before?
Your Confused Friend,

Kristine M., age 13

I noticed that some people have flags on their cars and some don't. I think the
people who don't are waving them in their hearts.

—Victoria L., age 5, weeks after the 9/11 attack on the United States

Kristine's question to the president has no simple answer.

Young Victoria was observant and innocently asked her dad, Tom, about why all the flags were suddenly appearing on people's cars and mailboxes. It is up to parents to provide the kinds of answers that will help their children understand, cope, and feel as safe and contented as possible.

The SAFE approach to communication gives you general guidelines to follow when talking to kids about sad or fearful events. If you review those guidelines you will develop a good, intuitive "feel" for how best to respond to your children. No doubt you'll have to think on your feet as children's questions can be unexpected and disarming.

This chapter will try to answer some of the more pointed questions children of any age might ask. The answers provided are not necessarily the only good ones.

Reviewing these may prevent you from being taken off guard and help you to respond with interest and effectiveness.

Guidelines

1. Get to the point. Answers of three or four sentences are sufficient for most questions. Longer answers may confuse or bore children and may cause them to avoid asking a follow-up for fear of having to sit through another speech.

2. Don't give grisly details. Don't be dramatic. Be truthful while emphasizing hope.

3. Get feedback. Ask, "What do you think about what I just said?" (The *S* in SAFE suggests you *search* out hidden concerns.) Probe a little if you think that your child is still uneasy. For example, a straightforward answer to the question "What is terrorism?" may miss the underlying question, which could be *"Is this family in danger from terrorism?"* (Key Point: Most underlying concerns a child might have will be about safety or fear of separation from a parent.)

4. End the conversation by saying, "Thanks for bringing that up. Those were good questions. Come to me anytime you have more questions."

Common Questions during an Uncommon Time

1. What is terrorism?

Terrorism comes from the word *terror*—which means very scary and frightening. If something is extremely frightening we say it is "terrifying." Terrorism happens when a person or groups of people try to frighten others by doing very bad and violent things to them. A terrorist is someone who might blow up a building just so he can frighten people.

2. Why do terrorists want to be violent and scare people?

What they do is very wrong. They do it because they don't like certain laws or they don't like how some people live their lives. They want to change the way people live by making them afraid to live their lives normally.

3. America is at war. Are Americans in danger?

The war that America is fighting is mostly happening in other countries. Yes, some terrorists have done some things that have hurt Americans, but I believe that we are safe. You won't see enemy soldiers in our town or in our country.

4. Adults always tell kids not to fight. Why do grown-ups go to war?

You're right. Grown-ups often fight when they shouldn't. Nobody wants to go to war. But if other people are trying to kill people in our country or put an end to our freedom we have to protect ourselves. If we go to war to protect ourselves we can save lives. The best thing to do is to pray that there will not be a need for wars in the future and that any wars happening now will end soon.

5. Will there be a nuclear war?

Nobody wants a nuclear war. There has never been one. Not every government has nuclear weapons. Our government is doing all it can to protect our country from any nuclear war and many other governments are doing the same thing.

6. When I grow up can I be a soldier or a police officer and kill the bad guys?

Soldiers and police officers are very brave. We need them to protect our cities and our country. But the best soldiers and police officers don't want to kill other human beings unless they have to. Yes, you could be soldier or officer some day. But I hope you never have to kill anybody.

7. Will terrorists bomb our buildings or crash our planes again? If I go on a plane, will it be hijacked?

Some terrorists might want to do that. But the government has learned better ways to protect us. The police are always looking for the terrorists and they have arrested many of them. It is much harder for terrorists to hurt us today than it was before. I wouldn't let us get on a plane if I believed we would be hijacked.

8. But they still could bomb us again, right?

Yes, they could. It is impossible to protect everybody at all times. But it won't be easy for them to hurt us. And if they do try to bomb us again I don't believe that anyone in our family will get hurt or killed.

9. How worried are you it will happen again?

I'm a little bit worried. I'm not worried that we will get hurt but I'm worried that somebody else will. The terrorists want us to worry. That way, they know they are upsetting us even when they are not really hurting us.

10. Did the people feel a lot of pain when the building fell on them or when their plane crashed?

Most people were probably killed instantly which means they really didn't have any time to feel pain. It is possible that some people who died when the planes hit their building did not die right away. Those people might have felt some pain. However, injuries that are very sudden and severe often don't hurt as much as we think they would. Our brain can do things to help keep the pain small.

11. What is anthrax?

It is a disease that certain animals such as cows usually get. Most animals are vaccinated, which means they get a shot to protect them from getting the disease. Even if they are not vaccinated, it is hard for animals to get the disease.

12. Why were people dying and getting sick from anthrax?

Some bad people wanted others to get sick from anthrax so they put some in envelopes and mailed them. The good news is that doctors know how to tell if someone has anthrax and medicines work very well in treating it. The people who died got the disease at a time when doctors did not know to look for anthrax as the cause for their illness. Most people will never be exposed to anthrax and will never get anthrax.

13. What if people in our city get anthrax? Can we get it, too?

Anthrax is not contagious. You cannot get it from being next to someone who has it. If someone in our city gets anthrax, doctors will give that person medicine to cure it. Also, the police will then look to see where the anthrax came from. Anybody who might have been near the anthrax will be given medicine to prevent them from getting sick.

14. Kids at school say we have to get a shot so we won't get small pox and die. What's small pox?

Small pox is a serious disease. When I was little I got a shot that kept me from getting small pox. Today, all kids in America gets shots to protect them from getting diseases like chicken pox and measles. They stopped giving shots for small pox because the disease went away. Now, the government thinks there is a chance the disease might come back so they want us all to be protected.

15. Everybody says not to worry and that we are safe. Then why is my class trip cancelled?

Yes, that is confusing. Many schools still have their school trips. Some don't. The truth is that parents and schoolteachers do believe we are safe. However, some people want to wait a while longer before school trips are allowed just to be extra safe. Most likely school trips will start up again next year.

16. If we are safe, why don't you want to fly in a plane?

You're right. It sounds like I am saying one thing but doing another. Sometimes people are afraid to do things even though they know they'll be okay. For example, when we went to the amusement park last year, some people were afraid to ride on the roller coaster even though it was safe and there were no accidents. Remember when our neighbor was afraid of our dog even though we knew our dog was friendly? It takes time for people to feel calm about some things. Hopefully I'll be ready to fly on a plane soon.

17. You keep saying we are safe, but people who thought they were safe were killed by bombs or by planes or by anthrax. How can you be so sure we are safe?

When I say we are safe I don't mean that everybody is always safe. Accidents happen, for example, and sometimes people will do bad things and hurt other people. But the truth is very few people in our country will be hurt by war or terrorists. We can live our lives as we normally do and we will be safe.

18. What is the government doing to protect the citizens?

The government has spies and FBI agents who find out about terrorist attacks before they even happen. That way they can prevent them. The government is working with other countries to capture all of the terrorists. The government has sent warplanes and soldiers to countries to fight terrorists. The President has promised that the government will defeat terrorism but it may take many years.

19. There are kids on TV who live in places like Afghanistan. They are getting killed. Some don't have any parents. Who takes care of them?

One of the sad things about war is that innocent people, such as little children, can get killed. Or, the parents of the children can get killed and the children become orphans. For a while, those kids will have difficult lives because it is hard to be cared for when your country is being bombed. But America wants to help rebuild the country and build places where these children can live. Let's hope that happens soon.

20. Why do kids bring guns to school and shoot people?

That has happened several times in the past few years. It is a very sad and scary thing. But it is also extremely rare. The kids who do the shooting are very unhappy and usually very angry. They feel that most people don't like them so they want to get back at them and hurt them. While many kids get angry and many kids can feel upset that others don't like them, it is only a very few who have actually used guns to hurt people. Schools are now doing more things to make sure that guns and other weapons are not brought into the schools. Also, teachers and school counselors are trying to help any child who feels angry so that child won't hurt anybody.

21. Could I ever get kidnapped?

It extremely unlikely. That is why I always tell you to stay near me when we go to the mall or the park. That is why I tell you not to talk to strangers and not to go with anybody—even someone you know—unless I give you permission. It is unusual for a child to be kidnapped but it does happen. Sometimes when parents are divorced and not living together, one parent will kidnap the child. The child is not in danger then but he or she will be upset because of missing the other parent.

Many stores use video cameras so they can tape the people coming and going. That way if someone tries to kidnap a child, he might be seen on camera and will be easier to find.

22. My friend at school is sad because someone in her family got killed. What can I do to help?
Wanting to be of help shows you that are a kind and compassionate person. You can let your friend talk to you about she is feeling. You can ask her how she's doing every once in a while. You can let her know that you understand why she is sad and that you'll always be her friend. Sometimes, kids who have a loved one who died get jealous of their friends whose loved ones are still alive. If your friend ever acts mean because she is jealous, try to understand. You can tell her not to treat you that way but you can also try not to take it personally.

23. Some bullies at school tease kids in my class. I feel bad for the kids that get teased. What should I do?
That's a great question. Most schools have bullies. Bullying is wrong and teachers and parents should know about it so they can stop it. One thing you can do is tell a teacher about it. Another thing you can do is go up to kids who are being bullied and let them know that you feel bad and that they don't deserve to be bullied. Bullies don't treat everyone bad. If they don't treat you bad you might even go up to the bully when he isn't busy and ask him to stop. If you see someone getting teased or bullied, never laugh at the person being teased. Never tease a person just because others are doing it.

24. Why did Daddy have to die?
Nobody knows why people have to die at the time that they do. Some people die when they are young. Most people die when they are old. It is always sad when people die. Daddy didn't want to die now. He wanted to be here with you and me. We both will miss him. But I believe his spirit is in heaven and that he sees us and always loves us.

25. Why didn't God stop the bad people? I thought he loved us?
That's a terrific question. Many grown-ups have asked that question and a lot of people can't figure out an answer that seems right. But I'll give you what I think is a good answer.

First of all, I believe that God does love us. He loves us as much as it is possible to love us. He wants us to love him. He could force us to love him but that wouldn't be true love. True love happens when we have a choice to love somebody or not but we love that person anyway. For example, you love your dog. But you don't love the dog that lives down the road. You could learn to love that other dog but you might choose not to try. Some people will choose to not love God. God doesn't want us to hurt people. But he allows it to happen so people can learn that hurting others is wrong.

Ten More Good Answers

Children won't always ask questions but they still might want answers. Sometimes they'll make passing comments that include hidden questions—questions you might easily overlook or minimize. Adults do this a lot when they don't wish to be direct. (For example, the comment, "It's hot in here" might really be asking the question, "Would you turn up the air conditioner?")

Similarly, a child who says, "I don't want to go to school" might really be concerned about a test, or bullies, or is worried that something bad will happen to his parents while he is away. Especially during stressful times, don't presume to know what your child's comments mean. Find out.

Comment #1: *I don't want to go to school.*

Say:

I'd like to hear your reasons.

Kids feel that way once in a while. Why don't you want to go?

I wonder if it has anything to do with _____? I know that's been on your mind.

Some kids have some worries and fears about school. Do you?

Don't Say:

Tough. You're going. (Yes, your child will probably go. Find out what the concerns are.)

I don't care. You know you have to go.

You don't mean that.

Comment #2: *I'm still afraid.*

Say:

Tell me more about that.

What can happen that might make you feel less afraid?

Do you feel less afraid than before or the same amount?

Fear doesn't always go away quickly. What scares you the most?

Don't Say:

You'll get over it.

Your brother isn't afraid. Why are you?

Don't be a baby.

Comment #3: *I don't want you to go on your business trip.*

Say:

I'd like to hear why you feel that way.

I'm wondering if you're worried about my safety?

What could I do when I'm away that would make you feel less worried? Would you like me to call you a couple of times a day?

What is the worst fear you have?

Don't Say:

Don't worry. I won't be gone long. (Too dismissive.)

I have to go. That's the way it is. (This comment tends to cut off conversation. Try to find out your child's concerns.)

If I don't go I might get fired. Then we wouldn't have any money. You wouldn't want that, would you? (No guilt trips.)

Comment #4: *Some kids in my class are afraid to fly in planes. Some aren't.*

Say:

That's understandable. What are your feelings?

How would you feel if I told you we were flying in a plane tomorrow?

What helps you to not feel as afraid as some of your classmates? (Or, what could happen that might help you and some of your classmates to feel less afraid?)

Don't Say:

It's dangerous to fly.

There's no reason to worry about flying. (Anxiety about flying is normal after hijackings or crashes. Trying to gently understand your child's concerns is far better than dismissing those concerns.)

Don't listen to what other kids are saying.

Comment #5: *Sometimes I don't think I'll live long enough to be an adult.*

Say:

What's been happening to make you think that?

What's different about those times when you think more positively?

What could happen that would make you feel more hopeful? What could happen that would make you feel less hopeful? (It is disturbing to hear your son or daughter make such a comment but take time to understand the reasons before you try to talk your child out of that belief.)

Don't Say:

Don't talk like that.

That's silly. Of course you'll grow up to be an adult.

You worry too much.

Comment #6: *People are too violent.*

Say:

I agree. What makes you say that?

Yes, some are. Is there something particular that happened that made you think that?

I wonder if you're worried about violence happening to you or someone you know?

Don't Say:

Not everybody is. (That's true but you miss the point. Explore your child's concerns about violence.)

You watch too much news.

There have always been violent people.

Comment #7: *I can't get to sleep. (Or, My stomach hurts.)*

Say:

That's no fun. Is something on your mind?

Sometimes we can't get to sleep (our stomachs hurt) when we're worried or upset about something. Are you worried?

Want to sit with me and talk?

Don't Say:

Try harder to sleep./Lie down and your stomach will feel better. (Search for hidden concerns instead.)

Try reading. That always makes me tired./You probably ate something you shouldn't have.

You're just like your father.

Comment #8: *I hope the terrorists die.*

Say:

A lot of people feel that way. What makes you say that?

What worries you the most about them?

What will happen if many of them do die?

Some people think they should just be put in jail for the rest of their lives. What do you say about that?

Don't Say:

You shouldn't be concerned about such things. (The child already is.)

I don't like it when you talk like that.

Yeah. Blow them all to bits. (That's a sentiment many people would agree with. However, I suggest you use this as an opportunity to understand your child better.)

Comment #9: *The news on TV is always bad.*

Say:

Yes, it can be. What did you hear last that bothered you?

You sound unhappy. What worries you the most of what you've heard?

Some kids watch the news and think that only bad things ever happen in the world, never good things. Do you ever feel that way?

Don't Say:

Just don't watch it.

The world seems to be more and more dangerous every day.

Get used to it.

Comment #10: *I feel sad when I think about what happened.*

Say:

That's understandable. Tell me more why you feel that way.

What's the saddest part of what happened?

I feel sad, too. Let's talk about it for a little bit.

Don't Say:

Try not to think about it.

You'll feel better soon. (That may be true. But your child is giving you a signal he or she wants to talk. Your comment closes off further dialogue.)

Think about happy things.

When my husband talks to our kids, especially about topics they are upset about, he gets impatient and seems to end the conversation sooner than I think is helpful. Any suggestions?

Often, one parent (usually the father but not always) likes to get to the "bottom line." He prefers to give solutions that solve the immediate problem ("Just don't play with that kid in your class if he bothers you") but that miss underlying concerns. Many men are less adept at showing empathy ("Gee, it must have been scary when _____") and are more comfortable teaching or setting rules. Typically, parents who converse like that also do the same with their partners, which can make for unsatisfactory communication.

Two points to remember are:

1. These men are attempting to make their child feel better but do not take the time to truly understand all that their child is saying.

2. They can learn alternative methods but they need to learn to be comfortable with their child's expression of emotion and not be so quick to talk the child out of his or her feelings.

It can help if parents say, *tell me more.* It allows the child to explore his feelings. It also helps if a parent "normalizes" a child's feelings by saying something like, *A lot of kids feel that way . . . It's normal to feel like that sometimes . . . I feel like that once in a while.* Normalizing feelings makes a child feel understood and changes the tone of the conversation from impatient listening to genuine under-standing. My book, *How to Say It to Your Kids: The Right Words to Solve Problems, Soothe Feelings, and Teach Values* gives many more suggestions on how parents can improve their communication skills.

Part Three

The Work Phase of Trauma, Tragedy, or Terror

It is not enough to talk to your children only during the immediate aftermath of some frightening event. After the event has passed, parents often engage in wishful thinking. *The kids are over it now . . . They don't need to be reminded of it . . . It didn't affect them directly . . . They were never that troubled to begin with so why keep bringing up the topic?*

The truth is, kids do still talk about upsetting events (such as shootings, terrorism, and violent storms) with their friends. Or, they think about them alone. The only way they have to put matters into proper perspective is to rely on their parents. If they believe that their parents don't wish to discuss a topic, the children will learn to grapple with it on their own. If they know that their parents are available for discussion and eager to offer comfort and answer questions, they will not only go the parents, they will feel more secure about their future.

Jason's dad died while doing his duty as a firefighter. He died two days before Jason's eighth birthday. It was a devastating loss. Jason and his two sisters couldn't stop crying in the days after their father's death.

Over the next several weeks, the family did their best to resume their day-to-day lives. Mom went back to work as a mortgage banker and the three kids were knee-deep in homework. But their days seemed unreal. Friends at school told them they felt sorry. But many kids said nothing. Jason watched classmates frolic during recess and wondered if he could ever feel that happy again. Thanksgiving was less than a month later. It would be a painful holiday, Jason imagined. Nothing would be the same. He had always looked forward to Thanksgiving dinner. Now he just wanted it to be over.

When the initial shock of trauma or loss starts to lessen and the immediate crisis has passed, families try to put their lives back together and participate in normal, everyday activities. They have entered the Work Phase. It is called "work" because of the emotional work required to put one foot in front of the other and go on with life at a time when the pain of loss is still fresh. During this phase, people try to incorporate the awful turn of events into their lives. The memory of the loss or trauma is still strong. Typically, people worry if some similar event could occur in the near future.

The work involved in this phase is not a simple matter of dusting oneself off and plowing ahead. After a trauma or significant loss, one's beliefs about self, the world, and the future are often shattered.

Old Belief: Whatever happens in my day-to-day life, I can probably handle it.
New Belief: I can't handle everything as well as I once thought.

Old Belief: My part of the world is reasonably safe.
New Belief: My part of the world is more dangerous.

Old Belief: My future is fairly bright.
New Belief: My future is uncertain and a little frightening.

After a significant loss or trauma, mistrust may replace trust. Anxiety may replace contentment. Fear may replace hope. Most people live their lives believing they have a reasonable amount of say over what happens to them. But tragedy can make people feel helpless and out of control.

When the tragedy hits home, the meaning of one's life can turn upside down. One day you wake up as a parent with responsibilities to your family. Then tragedy strikes—say, your spouse or child is killed—and the purpose to your life has been dramatically and forever changed. When hijacked planes crashed into the World Trade Center and the Pentagon, Americans no longer felt as safe as they once did. They stayed home more; they spent less money, and companies laid off tens of thousands of employees. Use of prescription drugs for depression and anxiety skyrocketed. But over time Americans did their best to live normal lives, still shaken from the events of 9/11 but ready to press on.

Talking to Kids during the Work Phase

The Work Phase can last weeks, months, or years depending upon the severity of the loss or trauma and the coping resources one has available. How you talk to kids during this time can be affected by how well you are coping overall.

Guidelines:

1. Take stock of how the event has affected your life and perhaps changed you. What worries do you have about the future? These may be worries your children have, too. How are you feeling overall? The more depressed or anxious you are, the more likely your children will have concerns. Your depression and anxiety per se are not necessarily a problem for your kids. But they do need to see you managing your life as effectively as possible.

2. Some effects of loss or trauma do not show up until time has passed. A child who seems to be doing fine may falter at special times of the year such as birthdays, holidays, graduations, or during special achievements. Kids unaffected by some terrorist attack may act fine until they have to enter a tall building or go on a plane.

3. Anger may show up during the work phase. Children who've suffered a loss or who have to rearrange their lives may be angry and want revenge. On the positive side, displays of anger may mean that fears have subsided.

4. If you are divorced or separated, it will be more important to cooperate with parenting and for each of you to give consistent messages about what is happening in the world. If there is ever a time to put aside differences for the sake of the children, now is the time.

Bringing Up the Topic—Again (Even When You Don't Think It's Necessary)

14

Are you crazy?

—A five-year-old girl, who was supposedly shielded from hearing any news of the 9/11 terrorist attack, upon learning two months later that her parents planned on taking a family trip to New York City

On September 11th we worried about what would happen next. Still, almost two months later we don't feel safe. We are worrying about anthrax now. This is not peace. This is fearing every second of the day.

—Jesse R., eighth grade

You will not cause psychological harm to your child if you bring up memories of a painful or scary time. Yes, reminding children of the loss of a loved one who is missed during Christmas or Hanukkah might make them feel sad. Reminding them of a frightening event may make them a little scared. But those feelings were not newly created, they already existed. (If a child shows *significant* distress when memories of a tragedy are triggered, then the child would benefit from professional help.) Keeping the topic hidden away is never a solution.

Most often, discussing a painful or scary memory helps promote healing. It lets the child know that it's normal to still have concerns or worries and that talking about it openly is allowed. If in fact the kids are doing just fine, then the talk will be brief

105

and will correspond to other behavioral cues the kids have given that they are okay. It's a win-win situation.

In my experience, parents who feel that a child would be unnecessarily burdened by being reminded of some tragedy, usually are uncomfortable with strong emotions. They may have been raised to limit their expression of feelings. *It's not me*, they say. *It's not how I was brought up.* It is perhaps too much to expect these parents to easily converse with their children during difficult times. I suggest, however, that they at least give it a try—a little talking is better than none at all—and not confuse *their* need to keep emotions under wraps with their children's needs. They may find it useful to ask a spouse or relative to help the conversation along.

Bring it up when it's possible to have a conversation, not when time is scarce. You may have to ask pointed—rather than open-ended—questions for some kids to provide the information you want. Searching for hidden concerns (the "S" in SAFE) is very important during the Work Phase.

- It's been a month since the terrorist attacks. What do you or your classmates say about it these days?
- Do kids in school ever talk about the school shootings they saw on TV? What do they say?
- I remember you were feeling a little scared after it happened. How are you feeling these days? Better? The same? Or worse?
- When you think about what happened (whatever it may have been), what exactly do you think of? What parts are on your mind most of all?
- Is there anything about what happened that you can't get out of your mind no matter how much you want to?
- Are there certain times of day or places to be where you feel more upset? Less upset?
- If you were bothered by something that happened, would you be more likely to talk about it with someone or keep it to yourself?
- If the way you feel today is how you would always feel about what happened, would that be okay or would you want to feel better?
- What was your worst fear before it happened? What is your worst fear today?
- In what ways do you feel better today than you did immediately after it happened?

- Is there something you wish people understood about how you are feeling that some people don't understand?

- I've noticed you are sleeping better (or, your stomach doesn't hurt so much) since _____ happened. Are you feeling better, too?

- You haven't spoken about what happened in quite a while. When you think about it, what kinds of things do you think?

- If something like _____ were to happen again, how do you think you would feel?

Make some general speculations about your child's feelings.

- Some kids still feel upset weeks after things like _____ happen. Maybe you do, too.

- I've noticed you seem to enjoy being with your friends again. I'm thinking you are feeling a little better. Am I right?

- Your life has changed quite a lot since _____. Some kids would feel angry about that. What do you feel?

- Sometimes after a tragedy, kids wake up one day and just start to feel better. I'm thinking you've begun to feel better. Am I right? Is there any way that you haven't begun to feel better?

Make some references to yourself.

- I still feel _____. What about you?

- I think it's important that I ask you how you are doing from time to time. Okay?

- Sometimes I feel like talking about what happened. Sometimes I don't. How about you?

- If I were you right now I'd be thinking _____ and feeling _____.

Take time as a family to discuss how the upsetting event has affected family life and specific members of the family. If your family has been completely unaffected by some tragedy or terrorism, discuss how others might be coping.

- It's been a month since _____ happened. I've noticed that one way we've been affected is _____. I'd like to hear some of your thoughts about that.

- Some days have been harder for us than others. What do you think is the biggest change our family has had since _____ happened?

- We were all sad and upset when _____ happened a couple of months ago. Even though we didn't know anyone who was killed, do you suppose that the awful event has changed us in any way? Do you think, feel, or act any different today because of what happened?

- It must be hard for those people who lost their homes in the tornado. I wonder what it's like for them right now?
- It's great having us all together at dinner. I feel bad for those families who lost loved ones when the building collapsed. Do you ever think of what those people might be going through?

End the conversation on a positive note.

- I'm glad we talked about it.
- Let's talk about it again sometime.
- Whenever you want to bring it up again I'll listen.
- I feel better that we talked.

- You're not still bothered about _____, are you?
- Most people feel better by now. Do you? (Some kids, especially teenagers, won't want to think of themselves as different from most people and therefore may not give you an honest answer.)
- There's no reason to still feel bad.
- You have to learn to get over things.
- It's over now. We really don't need to talk about it anymore.
- Dad (or some other deceased loved one) wouldn't want you to still get upset.

I keep hearing people say "Kids are resilient." Isn't it true that we don't have to worry too much about how kids will cope? Won't they eventually get over losses and tragedy like most people do? Don't kids bounce back rather easily?

Undoubtedly, some kids go through major traumas or an extremely harsh childhood and yet seem to make it to adulthood with few scars. And yes, regardless of what calamity happens, most kids will grow up and get married and have jobs and raise their own children. From that perspective one might conclude that early upsetting events are not that influential. But the truth is different.

First of all, kids who are "resilient" and seem to bounce back from some harsh and traumatic event or from experiences such as poverty, do so in large part because they have at least one very caring and influential adult in their lives. It might be a parent, grandparent, or even a teacher. But someone goes the extra mile for that child and makes themselves available on a regular basis to talk and to make that child feel loved and protected.

Second, even if a child who experiences loss or trauma is able to avoid major symptoms and grow up to be a responsible adult, they often possess scars. They may simply feel incredibly sad that a loved one did not live long enough to see them grow up. They may have a hard time trusting, which can cause problems in their relationships. Kids who go through major losses often feel different from other kids. Without someone to talk to whom they trust, they may have to wrestle with those feelings alone.

Talking to kids over the many months following some major upsetting event is like keeping a wound from becoming infected. Eventually, the wound heals.

15

When Racial Prejudice Follows Terror

We are children of America
Big, tall, short, thin
Our skins of chocolate, sand, roses, and snow
None of us the same
All different
Hopefully, to be treated equally under the law
We are children of America

We are children of America
Taking care of our country—USA
Waving flags, singing "God Bless"
Not perfect
But trying our best
You may think life is easy, you have no idea
We are children of America

—Amber M., age 15

A friend of mine stood pumping gas the day after the Twin Towers collapsed when a man walked up to her and pointed at the attendant's office. "Do you think foreigners own this place?" he said, scowling.

"Whatever they look like," she said, "they're Americans."

The man huffed and walked away.

Incidents of assault against Arab persons in the United States dramatically increased after the terrorist attack on 9/11/2001. One way of overcoming anxiety and

110

fear is to get angry. Anger makes a person feel stronger and less helpless. Unfortunately, lashing out against innocent people with anger just adds to the complexity of the problems we are facing in the world. Besides, it's just plain wrong.

It leaves one with a sick feeling to watch newsreels of a Ku Klux Klan rally with children dressing up in robes spouting hate. After the World Trade Center and Pentagon devastation, men, women and children in some towns in the Middle East cheered in the streets while thousands of innocent Americans lay crushed under rubble.

To help keep our kids from forming racial or religious stereotypes, it isn't enough for parents to refrain from making bigoted statements. They need to teach that while bad people exist, no one race of people or religious group is inferior or evil. They need to teach that tolerance, respect, and human dignities are not mere words but ways of conducting one's life.

Research shows that by age five—and even as young as age three—children can exhibit social prejudice (but not the hostility that often accompanies prejudicial attitudes by adults). One study showed that children ages five through nine who scored in the "high prejudice" range changed their attitude significantly when they discussed their beliefs with children who scored low in prejudice. Talks that emphasized similarities among different groups rather than differences made a big impact on changing negative beliefs. Another group of researchers examined attitudes toward people with AIDS in children ages five through ten. These same students were examined again two years later after basketball star Magic Johnson had acknowledged he was HIV-positive. The publicity surrounding that admission seemed to help the students understand AIDS better. These kids also showed a decrease in prejudicial thinking toward a hypothetical child with AIDS.

One of the many legacies of terrorism and crime is that bigotry expands. One way that victims can overcome the feeling of helplessness that often accompanies tragedy and devastation is to become angry with those who hurt them. But if they're not careful, they'll become angry with those who *look like* those who hurt them, too.

If prejudice and bigotry has not been a topic in your house, the Work Phase of trauma or loss is often an appropriate time to raise it. **Use news reports on the topic as an opening to the discussion.**

- Have you heard of the words *prejudice* and *bigotry?* What do you think they mean?

- Some people in other countries were happy when Americans were killed. They think Americans are bad. What do you think about that?
- After the terrorist attack, some Americans felt angry with all Arabs. What would you say to those people who felt that way? (Fact: Arabs constitute only 10 percent of the world's Muslim population.)
- If someone didn't like you just because you had blue eyes, how would that make you feel?
- If a child in your class teased another child for having different color skin or for belonging to a different religion, what would think? Would you do anything?
- If someone in your school did a bad thing and people said that everyone in the school must be bad, too, how would you feel? What would you want to have happen?
- If someone in our family did a bad or wrong thing and people in our town said that all of us must do bad things, what would you think? How would you feel?
- Do you ever notice that some kids in your school (neighborhood) are treated differently because of the way they look?

If your child makes a bigoted or slanderous remark (teens will more likely act that way than younger children will) and you are shocked and upset at what you hear, don't shame your child so quickly that conversation breaks down. **It's important to show strong disapproval, but try to have a conversation where your views and your child's can be heard. Try to empathize with the underlying emotion even if when you disagree with the remark.**

- I'm really surprised to hear you say that. What makes you feel that way?
- I'm shocked at what I heard. I'm not sure you understand the full meaning of what you just said.
- I wonder who else feels the way you do?
- It bothers me that you said that. Is that what you really meant?
- Many people might agree with you. But I don't and this is why. . . .
- Sometimes kids repeat what other kids say because they want to fit in. It isn't always easy to disagree with friends or classmates in order to do the right thing.
- I don't blame you for feeling angry about what happened. Still, it's important for all of us not to blame a whole group of people for the actions of a few.

- I feel mad, too. But I don't agree with what you just said.
- Sometimes it's easy to feel mad at a whole group of people when something terrible happens. The harder thing to do is make sure you don't blame innocent people—but that's also the right thing to do.

- How dare you! I never want to hear you say such a thing ever again! (On the plus side, you've made your views crystal clear—and that is important. The question remains: Will your reprimand help your child to change prejudicial thinking? It might, but then again, your child may be put off by your strong reaction and future conversations about this may be avoided. Get your point of view across without shaming your child. It increases the odds he or she will continue the dialogue and help you each to understand each other.)
- You sound just like your grandfather.
- You're absolutely right.

If you hear your (probably older) child repeating a racial joke or mocking a group of people in some way, say:

- Please don't repeat jokes like that. You may not realize it but you are making jokes at other people's expense.
- Many kids your age like to tell jokes like that. But I'd like you to think about what you are really saying. It's really a form of bigotry.
- Our ethnic background is _____. People have made jokes about our background, too. Yes, some jokes can be funny if they are intended as good-natured fun. But some jokes are meant to make fun of others and put them down. That's wrong.
- You never know when you say a joke like that if you are offending a listener.
- I've told jokes like that, too. Then I realized I was doing it so I could feel important or well liked and I wasn't thinking about the fact that I was putting down a whole group of people.

If your child or teenager responds to your comments by saying such things as:

Everyone is prejudiced at least a little.
It's just a joke.
No one else seems to mind.

You reply:

You're probably right. I think it's important that we try to reduce our prejudices as much as possible. Please think about what I'm saying. We can talk more about it later.

I'm glad to hear that you didn't really mean it. Still, jokes can be hurtful to some people. Please don't tell jokes like that anymore.

I just want you to be aware of what you are saying. I want you to be aware that our words can hurt people as much as our actions can.

I have good kids, really. And I don't make bigoted remarks. But my father-in-law does and I don't know how to handle those situations. My husband says not to make a big deal out of it because I might stir up trouble. What should I do? If I don't say anything to my father-in-law, what effect will that have on my kids?

You seem to be describing a classic double-bind: if you talk to your father-in-law he and your husband may get annoyed. If you don't, your kids are exposed to bigoted attitudes that go unchallenged. Hopefully, your children's attitudes will be more influenced by you than by their grandfather. At a minimum you need to tell your children that their grandfather's comments are wrong and hurtful. I would brainstorm with your husband what, if anything, he might be willing to say to his father. For instance, he may be unwilling to challenge his dad by saying something like: *Dad, I don't like your attitude. Please don't talk like that in front of my kids.* (By the way, the more bigoted a person is the more likely he or she is difficult to get along with in general. Your husband may have been criticized or intimidated by his dad over the years, which is the main reason he does not wish to cross him now.) Still, your husband might be willing to confront his dad more gently. *Dad, your grandkids and I love you. But could you wait until the kids are out of the room before you say those things?* Even though your husband is reluctant to challenge his father, it is possible that he has his limits, too. Find out if there is any bigoted remark his father might say that would force him to speak up to the man.

You might have influence by confiding in your mother-in-law. She is probably well accustomed to the family politics and may be willing to speak to her husband about his manners without making you the villain.

If all else fails you might be forced to reduce the amount of time your kids spend with their grandfather. If they love him and he is generally good to them they should not be deprived of his company. I would also read stories to your children about bigotry on a more regular basis so your views on the subject are clear to them.

Tips for Divorced Parents on Helping Kids Cope During Uncertain Times

16

The divorce taught my kids that life is not always predictable and that loss is a part of life. That troubled me. So I made a point of showing them that life can be wonderful, too. Then the world went crazy with terrorism and now I wonder if my kids can ever believe and trust in anything again.

—Madeline G., divorced mother of three

Divorced parents have their work cut out for them. Life is almost always more stressful after a break up. Access to the children is more limited and differences in parenting style may become accentuated as couples go their separate ways. When the world becomes a scary place, divorced parents need to be especially attuned to how well or poorly their kids are coping and be willing to cooperate in parenting.

During loss or troubling times, divorced parents may react more extremely than is helpful. They may underplay the events and hold the attitude that "My kids are doing fine"—not because the kids really are fine and unaffected, but because the parents are already too stressed and need to believe the kids are okay. Or, parents may over-compensate and assume that their kids are more affected than they actually are.

A more troublesome situation occurs when one parent accuses the other of over- or underreacting. Then, old marital wounds reemerge under the guise of what's best for the child. When separated or divorced parents are reacting more to each other than to an honest assessment of their children's needs, the children lose.

Divorced parents often mean well when they struggle to cooperate with parenting.

But anger at each other or guilt over the impact of the divorce on the kids can derail cooperation and give rise to stubborn standoffs: *You're wrong . . . You're not thinking of the kids . . . Don't you care what happens to them? . . . You're babying them . . . You always make mountains out of molehills . . . You always want to pretend the kids are doing just fine . . . Other mothers (fathers) would do it differently. . . .*

It is predictable that many divorced parents will disagree on how to talk to their kids about things like terrorism, war, and the death of a family member. One parent may think it unnecessary to have such discussions, or to have them only if the children initiate them. The other parent may believe it is important to raise the topic periodically and to look for hidden concerns. Another complication is remarriage. A stepparent may have different ideas than a parent on talking to kids about troubling times. In both cases the children deserve parents who are involved and responsive to their needs.

How to Say It to Your Ex

Before talking to your children, it might help to have a conversation with your former spouse (and/or your new spouse). If you and your ex have had a positive and cooperative relationship so far since the divorce, hopefully that will continue. However, if family members have been strongly affected by recent troubling events or perhaps were victims—emotions may run high and cooperation may get strained.

State your views on how to talk to the children. Be open to suggestions.

- I noticed the kids were worried when they saw the news on TV. I'd like to ask them how they feel and try to answer their questions. What are your thoughts?

- I don't feel comfortable giving them simple reassurances because they are old enough to know that bad things can happen. I'd like to point out the ways I think they will be safe and cared for. What do you think?

- The kids seem to be okay and they haven't mentioned anything about the terrorist attack. I'm thinking I'll just wait until they raise the topic before I talk to them. What do you think is best?

Don't be dogmatic and presume to know better than your ex. Don't say things like:

- You must cooperate with me on this.

- It's essential that you talk to them when you see them this weekend. If you don't they will get the message that you don't care.

- You're wrong to talk about it with them. You'll just make them more upset.

- I'll do it the way I want to do it. Don't tell me what I should or shouldn't do.

- I'm going to tell the kids that you don't like talking and they can't count on you for that.

- I'm going to tell the kids that you are making too much out of this event and that you shouldn't be asking them so many questions.

If you don't completely see eye to eye, try to find something about your ex's point of view that makes sense. Point out what you agree with before you state what you disagree with.

- That makes sense. Although I'd also like to try it this way. . . .

- I see what you mean.

- I agree with you on that part.

- You might be right about that. I'm not sure.

- Maybe neither of us knows what's really best until we try something. Let's start by saying _____ and seeing what happens. How does that sound?

- I can see why you might feel that way. Do you agree that my way makes some sense, too?

- Is it possible that we both might be right, at least in part?

- I'm willing to try it your way the first time. But if it doesn't seem to help I'd like us both to try a different way.

If your ex refuses to see your view, state how you intend to handle the situation (without getting mean).

- I guess we disagree and we each feel strongly about how we feel. I'll handle it the way I think is best and you'll handle it your way. If my way isn't working, I'll certainly consider doing it your way.

- I just cannot agree to do it your way. If the kids wonder why you are handling it differently than I am, I won't criticize your method. I'll tell them you are doing what you think is best and that I am, too.

- I wish we could agree on this. On some matters I'd be willing to go along with your ideas just to keep things pleasant. But this situation is too important. I have to handle it the way I think is best. I hope you understand.

Don't Say:

- I've come to expect this sort of thing from you.

- You never want to listen to reason.

- Don't expect me to cooperate next time you need a favor. (The kids are better off when you and your ex cooperate as often as possible.)

If you and your mate are able to cooperate at least partly, say something nice.

- This can work. Thanks.

- I appreciate what you are doing. I know you haven't always agreed with everything that we've had to do.

- It's really nice when we can agree.

- I'm very appreciative.

- It means a lot to me that we can work together like this.

- It's clear to me that you want what's best for the kids, even if you and I don't always agree on what is best.

PHRASES TO USE ───────────────────

Thanks.	That means a lot.
I see your point.	That makes sense.
I want to hear your views.	Can you agree at least partly with me?
It was nice when you . . .	You were right about . . .
That worked out nicely.	I was wrong about . . .
Call me if you have questions.	What do you think?

PHRASES TO AVOID ───────────────────

You always . . . You never . . .	Just forget it.
You're completely wrong.	You don't care.
We'll see about that.	Just try it. I dare you.
The kids will see right through you.	You're only doing this to hurt me.
You should . . .	If you really cared you would . . .
It's about time you cooperated.	I don't care what you think.

INSTEAD OF SAYING:	SAY:
You don't understand.	What I'd really like you to understand is . . .
You're wrong.	I disagree.
Have it your way.	Let's try it your way first, then my way.
If you cared you would . . .	What about my view do you agree with?
You always . . . You never . . .	I'm hoping that this time you will . . .
You're so stubborn.	It's frustrating when we reach a roadblock.
You don't care about the kids.	It's sad that we can't always agree.
Tough, I'm doing it anyway.	I need to do what I think is best.
You never listen to me.	Is there something I don't fully understand?
You win. I don't have the strength to argue.	I'll think about it. Let's talk later.
It's about time you agreed with me.	Thanks.

Talking to Your Kids

If you are divorced, separated, or remarried, you need to consider that fact when talking to your kids during troubling and scary times. If the separation is recent, for example, your kids may have more difficulty dealing with world events because they are still trying to adjust to the new family life. And as discussed in the last section, how your kids handle your conversations may depend, in part, on how well you and your ex (or your new mate) are cooperating.

Broadly speaking, you and your ex will either be in sync when talking to your kids or you will differ in your approach. Never demean your ex when talking to your kids. It makes no sense to offer comfort and reassurance to kids during scary times while simultaneously demeaning your partner. That only diminishes your child's sense of trust.

If you and your ex agree on how to talk to your kids, mention that to your children. It reaffirms that you both, as parents, are cooperating.

- Your father and I think it's important to talk with you about what is happening in the world these days.

- Your mom suggested that you and I talk about the school shootings (plane crashes, terrorist attacks, neighborhood crimes, and so on) that you've heard about. I agree with her.

- I'm glad that your dad spoke with you about what happened.

- Mom told me that she asked how you were feeling about _____. I'm glad she did that. We both care about what's happening with you.

If you and your ex don't agree on how to talk to the children don't criticize your ex.

- *Don't say:* Your dad refuses to discuss this with you but I think it's important.

  Say instead: I think this is important to discuss.

- *Don't say:* Your mom doesn't understand what's best.

  Say instead: Although Mom has a different point of view, this is what I think is best. . . .

- *Don't say:* I don't care what your mother (father) thinks. This is what I think.

  Say instead: Your mom and I don't agree on this so I'll tell you what I think is important.

- *Don't say:* Don't listen to your father (mother, stepmother).

  Say instead: It's probably confusing that your dad and I disagree about what to say to you. We both want what's best for you but we don't always agree on what's best.

- *Don't say:* Tell your father that you agree with me and that you want to talk to him about what has happened in the world.

  Say instead: I'll be happy to tell your father that you'd like him to talk to you about what has happened. But if he doesn't think it's a good idea he may choose not to talk.

- *Don't say:* I can't believe he said that to you.

  Say instead: That isn't what I would have said. Let's talk about it now and maybe I can answer some of the questions you still have.

- *Don't say:* I can't believe he said nothing about it to you.

  Say instead: I can ask him to talk to you. In the meantime, I'm willing to talk to you about it. I think it's important.

If your child says:

Mom told me that you never want to talk about this kind of stuff.

Dad says that you don't know what you are talking about.

Mom says she doesn't want to discuss it and that if I have any questions I should talk to you.

You reply:

I'm not that much of a talker. But I think that what happened is very important and should be talked about.

I guess we disagree on what is best. I do know what I am talking about and I'd like to talk now.

Okay. I'm happy to do that. How does that sound?

I'm a divorced father of two teenagers. I try to see them as often as possible but they sometimes want to be with their friends rather than with me. We talk on the phone or via e-mail, but I feel I've been slowly losing touch with them. When major world events happen like the terrorist attack on New York City, I want to connect with them but I don't feel I'm succeeding. I feel more and more irrelevant. Am I wrong to think this way? What can I do so my kids will know they can turn to me for anything, especially when life gets scary or difficult?

Actually, many parents who are still with their spouses feel less connected to their teenagers. Part of growing up is trying to act independently. Thus, teens may seem less affected by world events or less inclined to want to talk about it with their parents. However, their process of independence is made workable only if they have a stable, reliable home base to return to—even if that means separate homes for you and your ex. Teens need the safety and security that "home base" and parents can bring them— even if they don't acknowledge the importance of those things.

Never conclude that you are unimportant to your teens. Never diminish the role that you play. Ask people whose parent had died when they were still teenagers or young adults. They will tell you that the loss was devastating. Despite protests to the contrary, teens know deep down that they don't have all the answers. Your presence in their life would be missed if you pulled back because you wrongly concluded that you were not that important to them.

I suggest you talk about the world events anyway. Your kids will be receptive or not, but they will know that you care about them and that you are available for conversations. Don't forget affection whenever possible. Always show an interest in things your teens are involved in. On weekends you might spend with your kids, it's okay to invite their friends along. Occasionally do something exciting that a teenager might enjoy other than the usual rent-a-movie or go-to-the-mall activity. See a live play, go rafting, take a drive to an amusement or theme park, get tickets to a concert or professional ballgame. Talk to their friends about a more interesting topic other than mere chitchat. Your children's friends, in order to be polite, may actually talk more about a subject with you than they would to their own parent. If your kids' friends enjoy your company, your children may actually find you more appealing, too.

Feeling Guilty After a Loved One Has Died

17

Everything at home looks the same. But nothing feels the same.

—Sam R., 9, whose dad was killed by a drunk driver while on his way to see Sam's school concert

Weeks and months after a loved one has died, people still grieve. If the death was sudden and unfair, such as when a loved one is murdered or dies in a horrific accident, the pain of loss can be compounded by images of what the person went through in the moments before death. A sudden death of a loved one is a shock to the nervous system. *I still can't believe it happened* people say. *I can't get it through my head that she's gone.* Then there is the pain of guilt. Survivors feel guilty over past wrongdoings, for never having said they were sorry, for never having said "I love you" enough. Sometimes they feel guilty for being alive. *He wouldn't have died if only I had . . .*

Children grieve in waves. One minute they are sad and crying, the next they are chatting on the phone with a friend or playing games. Younger children possess "magical thinking" and believe that if they *think* about something and then it happens, that they caused it. That can make them feel guilty should something bad happen. Older kids and teens often act disrespectfully to parents or at least they *think* angry thoughts. They usually feel guilty about those thoughts if the parent dies unexpectedly.

The task for parents and caregivers during the Work Phase is to help the children adjust to the loss so that normal activities, such as coming home from school or going to bed at night or having dinner, are not filled with painful memories and unnecessary guilt.

How to Say It

Hasty reassurances that there is no need to feel guilty are usually insufficient, though such comments have their place. Don't rush in to make your child feel better without first trying to understand the nature of the guilt feelings.

- I know what you mean. Many people feel guilt after someone dies. What do you feel guilty about?

- Why do you think what you did was so bad?

- Do you think what you did made _____ unable to forgive you? Or do you know you are forgiven but you just wish it hadn't happened? (Draw a distinction between guilt—which means *I'm bad, I'm to blame*—and regret which means *I wish it didn't happen.*)

- Why do you think you are to blame for what happened?

- Yes, you did say (do) some things that you wish you had not said (done). I've said and done things, too, that I wish I hadn't. But I know that _____ loved us and wasn't really that bothered by what we did.

- If I stubbed my toe when I was bringing you your dinner, would it be your fault I stubbed my toe even though it wouldn't have happened if you weren't here? Is it your fault _____ died just because he was doing something for you when it happened?

- You seem to focus on the things you did that you regret, but you're not focusing on how much _____ (Mom, Dad, Grandpa, and so on) loved you.

- Do you remember any times when you did something wrong but _____ forgave you and loved you anyway? Why does this time have to be any different?

- I remember when you did _____ to me. Even though I didn't like it I still loved you then and I love you now.

- Sometimes when we feel guilty we are just feeling very sad that something happened and we really aren't to blame. Maybe you are feeling sad and that's all.

- Sometimes when someone dies, kids feel they are to blame. They are never to blame. It is never a child's fault.

- If you did that to me and I later died, I know I would not be hurt or angry. In fact, I would want you to remember me with love.

- When someone loves you the way _____ loved you, there is no room in his heart to stay angry.

- Say a prayer and tell her you are sorry. Let me know later how that makes you feel.

- Write her a letter and say you are sorry. You can read it out loud if you want. She'll get the message. And I know she will understand and she will smile.

Religious beliefs are important when coping with death. However, children might react wrongly to your message unless you make sure they truly understand what you are trying to convey. For example, after hearing about heaven they may want to die and go to heaven to be with the loved one. Or, they may feel so guilty that they will purposely misbehave because they feel they don't deserve to go to heaven.

Clarify that heaven is a wonderful place but that God wants us to live our lives until he decides it is time for us to die and be with him. Remind your child that everybody makes mistakes and occasionally does wrong things but that God is all-forgiving.

- When I tell you that _____ is in heaven with God, what do you think about that?

- Yes, I miss _____. I'd like to be with him. But it is important for me to live my life for as long as God wants.

- I believe that _____ is in heaven. Even though I know she is happy, I still wish she were here with us.

- If we are sorry for things we do that are wrong, God forgives us.

- Don't feel that way.

- Don't feel bad (sad). The people who died are in heaven and happy. (Don't make a child think that her feelings—which are normal—are inappropriate. A child may not understand how a loved one can be so happy if they are not with their surviving family.)

- There's no reason to feel guilty. (Try to understand the nature of the guilt. Explain that it is normal for many people to feel a little guilty but that doesn't mean they are responsible for the death or that the one who died no longer loves them. Love overcomes guilt.)

- It has been months since _____ died. I can't believe you still feel guilty.

- Maybe now you'll learn your lesson and think twice about saying hurtful things to others. (Making your child feel guiltier is cruel. If you want your child to somehow learn a lesson, say: *After* _____ *happened, there were things I wish I hadn't said or done, too. I know the person who died loves me completely. I know I'm sorry and I am forgiven. And I will try to be a better person, though everybody makes mistakes.*)

- God took _____ to heaven because she was such a good person and God wanted her with him. (Your child may then want to misbehave so God won't take him, too. Or, your child may try to be perfect and get very worried anytime he does something wrong for fear that wrongdoings will prevent him from ever entering heaven.)

Nobody in my family has ever been hurt or killed in some awful accident. Nothing scary has happened to any of us. But after we watched the news of major floods in the Midwest where many people died or lost their homes, my nine-year-old daughter acted overly nice to her siblings and me. I got the distinct impression she felt guilty about what happened in the Midwest when it was clearly not her fault. Am I imagining things?

It is not likely that she feels guilty about the floods. However, hearing about the devastation and loss of life may have triggered some guilt about other things she has done. Maybe she realized that tragedy and death could happen suddenly and that people she loves could die without her having a chance to say she's sorry. Maybe she realized for the first time that her parents are not invulnerable and she felt bad for having misbehaved in the past. Possibly a classmate is going through a rough time and she feels guilty for not having showed support or kindness to that person. I suggest you mention to her that she seems troubled by something ever since she saw news of the floods. If she doesn't admit to anything, you can suggest possibilities, *I wonder if you might be feeling bad about . . .* Even if she does not open up, she will know that you are available.

If you are separated, divorced, or widowed, your daughter may be feeling guilty about something related to that. Make some gentle inquiries.

Why Did God Let This Happen?

18

Where was God on September 11th?

—Robert G., age 11; phrase repeated by countless people.

The line outside the funeral home stretched for blocks. My son, a high school freshman, and I stood nearly three hours on a chilly night to pay our respects to an upper classman who died the day before. Grief-stricken teenagers kept a somber vigil. The deceased boy's parents graciously accepted the tears and embraces of the hundreds of people who offered their condolences. Over a six-month period three students from his school died in traffic-related accidents. Dear God, why?

While it is indeed a tragedy when someone is killed in a car accident, it is not terrifying. We've come to accept such accidents as awful realities that happen. But how do kids and teenagers react to these events? They may convince themselves that if the victim had worn a seat belt or driven more carefully the death would have been avoided. In other words, death is avoidable if you do the right things. But these losses often puncture a hole in a child's sense of safety. A fleeting glimpse of a profound truth is revealed—that life is precious and can be taken from us in a moment's notice—before he or she can patch that hole with illusions of immortality.

But auto accidents that kill children and teenagers are now happening in the wider context of anxiety, terror, and uncertainty. Kids see news reports of a child being kidnapped; perhaps they see the shopping mall video that shows the child being escorted by a stranger outside before the child disappears. Then stories like the Oklahoma City bombing—where innocent children died—and the Columbine school-shooting massacre filled headlines across the nation while pictures of planes exploding into buildings filled our eyes. Life is more uncertain than ever.

In the aftermath of loss or tragedy, many kids will have questions about why God lets bad things happen. For some, the answers will suffice. Older children, already feeling let down by a world they've discovered cannot be trusted, may question their belief in a Supreme Being.

Even parents who try to raise their children with religious beliefs and who attend religious services regularly, may avoid talking with their children about why God allows tragedy and evil. They avoid it because they don't have answers they feel comfortable giving. They avoid it because they want their kids to believe that God is good and loving. Raising the "Why?" question may cause some kids to doubt God's love.

The question of why God allows suffering and injustice has been asked for thousands of years. Do not worry about providing "the" answer. You simply need to give "an" answer. You need to show that one's personal belief in God is often tested and that true faith involves a willingness to believe even when there is reason to doubt. You need to show that it is normal and okay to get angry with God when tragedy strikes. You need to show your children that trying to learn about God's ways and discover his intent is a worthwhile, lifelong goal.

If tragedy has struck on a personal level, other adults may be questioning God's love while the children overhear those comments. Or, the children themselves might raise the question. **Don't end the discussion quickly simply because you don't have an answer you strongly believe in. Try to take a little time with your answers. Remember that your answers represent your (perhaps ever-changing) beliefs, not facts. Leave the topic open-ended and invite future discussions.**

If your child or teenager asks: *Why did God let this happen?*
You say:

- That is an important question but not an easy one to answer. I believe that bad people made a choice to hurt other people. God didn't want it to happen but he gives everybody the right to choose good or evil.

- What happened was an accident. God did not make it happen.

- I don't know why God allowed it to happen. It wasn't fair. But he allows many unfair things to happen. It is hard to understand why. What are your thoughts?

- Some people think that God allows bad things to happen because he wants us to love one another. One way we show love is helping others when bad things happen to them.

- Often, people only realize what is truly most important in life—learning to love and care for one another—after bad things happen.

- I'm not sure why. The collapse of the World Trade Center and the deaths of all the firefighters and police officers were awful. But after that happened, more people started to pray and go to church and help those in need. Maybe bad things happen so that we can do some good for the people who need help and get closer to God.

- I don't know for sure. We are Christians. Jesus suffered and died for us. His mother must have suffered when she watched him die. Yet so much good came from that as more people believed in God and in heaven.

- I don't know the answer. Maybe it is a question we should pray about.

- I think God gets sad when bad things happen. He doesn't want them to happen.

- God could probably make everything perfect for us so there would be no pain or suffering or death. But what he wants most is for us to love him—really love him. That means we have to be willing to love him even when things go wrong.

- God did not promise us happiness in this life. Only in the next life. We have to try to make our lives as faithful to God as possible, especially when bad things happen.

- God wants us to trust in him, no matter what happens. That is harder to do when bad things happen. Still, I try to trust him even during awful times.

If your children lost a loved one in some tragedy or is suffering in some way, they may lash out at God and your religious beliefs. That can be upsetting to parents who have tried to instill faith in their children. If your children are argumentative, don't directly challenge their point of view—after all, they are looking for an argument and not interested in a philosophical debate—and you'll fall into a trap. It is a mistake to immediately tell them they are wrong to feel that way. It is normal to feel angry with God after a tragic, unfair loss. Be kind, give them permission to feel angry and sad, and gently tell them that you are trying to hold on to your beliefs despite what happened.

If your child says:
God doesn't love us.

Say: It is normal to think that, especially when things are sad and bad things happen. I have thought that God doesn't love us. But I have also changed my mind. Now I believe he does love us, but I understand why you think he does not.

Don't Say: Stop saying that. Of course he loves us.

I don't want to believe in God anymore.

Say: You sound very hurt and angry. I know how you feel.

Don't Say: Then you won't go to heaven and see everyone you love. God will punish you.

I hate God.

Say: I know how you feel. It's hard to like him right now. It's okay to talk to him and tell him that you are angry at him. I'm going to pray to him and ask him to help us understand better.

Don't Say: That's a terrible thing to say! You will go to hell for saying that kind of thing! You better pray right now that God will forgive you.

It's stupid to believe in God after what happened.

Say: I see how angry you are. I can't blame you. Deep down I'm angry, too. I still believe in God, I just don't always understand his ways.

Don't Say: It's not stupid. You have a bad attitude.

I'm not going to church (synagogue, mosque) anymore.

Say: Many people feel the way you do. We will all be going to church as a family. But I don't expect you to participate much given how you are feeling. It's okay if you sit back and do nothing when we are there.

Don't Say: Don't talk to me in that tone. And yes, you will be going to church!

How can God be all-good if he let that happen?

Say: That's an important question. It is not easy to understand why God, who loves us, would let something awful happen. But I don't want to believe in God if he is not all good. Therefore, there must be a good reason why he lets bad things happen. Some people believe that God allows bad things to happen because he knows that people will pray to him and get closer to him when they are afraid or sad. When people are happy they often forget about him. Once they forget about him they may start doing more bad things.

Don't Say: Who knows . . . I don't want to discuss it . . . You shouldn't question God's actions . . . Maybe God really doesn't care about us.

During times of tragedy or loss, you as a parent may be struggling with your faith. You may be very angry with God. You may feel that God has abandoned you or that God should have intervened and protected you and your family since you had always tried to be faithful. Thus, if your child asks questions about God, you may be cynical and unable to help your child maintain a belief in God. Or, you may lash out at God within earshot of your child (or, perhaps another relative will lash out and it will be up to you to explain that behavior to your child).

If you are very angry at God (or another adult in the family is angry) and you are having a difficult time answering questions about God in a reassuring way, say:

• Right now I'm angry with God. I don't want to feel that way but I do. I hope to feel differently some day soon.

• It probably upsets you to see me (or Grandpa, Dad, Aunt Lily, and so on) so angry with God. I just don't understand why God lets bad things happen when we don't deserve it.

• Many people feel angry with God after something like this happens. But many people feel less angry over time. I hope to be one of those people.

• Grandpa is very angry with God because he thinks God should have done something to prevent _____ from happening. God understands Grandpa's feelings and hopefully Grandpa will feel less angry eventually.

Don't dismiss any of your child's questions simply because the answers are difficult. Don't lose sight of the way your tone and attitude can affect your child.

• Just ignore Grandpa when he says those things. He's just angry. (*Better:* Grandpa is angry with God because he feels God let him down. That's a normal feeling. I hope Grandpa eventually feels more at peace with what happened.)

• Who knows why God lets bad things happen? (Too dismissive.)

• Maybe God doesn't exist. Maybe people who believe in God or who believe that God loves us are just fooling themselves. (If this represents a change in your thinking, it is best to admit that you are angry and confused and to perhaps mention that you would like to still believe in a loving God.)

• It's wrong to question God. (Often, questioning God's judgment allows a person to understand God better. It is one way of deepening a relationship with God.)

I believe in God and I believe God is all-good and all-loving. But it is hard to understand why God allows tragedies to happen, especially to innocent people. Is there something I could say to myself that would help me to trust in God's love? If I have doubts, will those doubts transfer to my children? If they have doubts at an early age, will they be more likely to have doubts later on in life?

God can never be fully fathomed. And faith in God is built, in part, upon mystery. We are not showing true faith if we believe only because we have sufficient proof or evidence. True faith happens when we believe despite having reasons to not believe. I do not think it is harmful (spiritually or morally) to your children if you are struggling with your faith. If believers are honest, they will admit to grappling with doubts from time to time. I think it is important that you convey in words and in actions a desire to get closer to God despite your doubts. Should your doubts cause you to be less charitable toward others or to cause you to pray less or go to church less often, those behaviors will have an impact on your children. Your actions do speak loudly. Even if parents are religious, children often find religious beliefs and rituals boring and not very meaningful. However, when those children grow up and perhaps have children of their own, they often see things more clearly through their parents' eyes and understand the value of religion and spirituality.

People who believe in God tend to fall into one of two camps. One group views God as loving but detached; uninvolved in day-to-day human life. Thus, when bad things happen they do not blame God because they do not view God as playing an active role in humanity. The other group views God as more personal, more involved in one's life. They believe that God might answer prayers or perform miracles. But why God answers some prayers and not others remains a mystery. I have found it helpful to believe that God has a plan for each person. I believe that the plan is ultimately for our good. But since the greatest good is to spend eternity with God—not to be happy on earth—that plan may include loss or suffering. Let's face it, if we live long enough and love hard enough we will inevitably face some sort of suffering. Pray for the strength to trust that no matter what happens to you, God has a plan for you personally that is good. When you think of it that way, then even when tragedy strikes—and even if that tragedy was not what God wanted—you might find it possible to persevere knowing that God's plan for you still exists and is for your ultimate good.

When Your Child Is Angry After Tragedy or Loss

I believe that this planet is ridiculous because of how poorly we treat our world and the beings on it. Because we don't like someone or their race, should we bomb him or her? Should we take their life and cause a war?

—Nicole R., age 13

"I'm a cop," the man explained to me. "I haven't had any close calls, thank God, and my kids never seemed to worry too much about my safety. But when terrorists hit New York and Washington, my kids became more concerned. My son is nine. He's still angry at the terrorists. He says things like 'Kill them all!' I worry about him."

During the Work Phase of trauma or loss, weeks or months (even years) after the awful event happened, anger can linger. Hopefully, it will fade and not be intrusive. But it might persist. Anger is a part of grief. Tragedies always seem unfair and unfairness makes most people angry. Anger also makes people feel empowered at a time when bad things have happened that were out of their control. Some people prefer feeling anger instead of helplessness.

Your children may express anger after there has been sad or scary news. They may express it mildly and briefly, or it may show up periodically for quite some time. If a loss affected them personally, it is normal for them to express anger. Complete lack of anger might indicate that a child is withdrawing or keeping feelings to himself. Intense anger that is frequently expressed suggests that the child may have underlying fears or concerns that need to be addressed. Regardless, anger should be allowed and viewed as a possible clue to underlying concerns.

Whether or not some tragic world or local event personally affected your child, he or she may express some anger over it. Try to elicit more information about why he or she feels that way. Don't criticize the feeling. Remember the SAFE approach.

- You sound kind of angry. Many people feel that way about what happened.

- You have strong feelings about what happened. What makes you the most angry?

- What other ways do you feel?

- What ways do you think other people feel, especially those who were personally affected?

- I don't blame you for feeling angry. What bothers you the most about what happened?

- Some people might feel angrier than you. Why might they feel that way? Some people feel less angry than you do. Why?

- You don't seem as angry about it as you were last week. What changed? Do you feel less worried about something?

- You seem angrier than you were last week. Are you? What changed?

Underneath anger is often fear of future loss, fear of lack of control over events, and hurt over injustice. Search for these issues with older children and teenagers.

- Some people get angry over things like this because they worry it could happen again. Is that true for you?

- Some people get angry about what happened because it was so unfair. Sometimes they are angry about past unfair events in addition to the most recent event. What do you think about that?

- Some people get angry because they feel let down. Do you ever feel let down by anyone?

If the child is very angry and yet was not personally affected by what happened, the event has probably triggered some other concern. Search for possibilities.

- You're right to be angry. What happened was very sad (wrong, tragic, unexpected, and so on). But your anger is strong and that makes me wonder what else you might be angry about?

- Does this awful thing that happened remind you of anything else that has happened that you might also be angry about?
- Sometimes there is some fear or worry underneath anger. Is there something that worries you?
- If you could make a speech and the whole world would be able to listen to you, what would you want the people of the world to understand?
- Is there something on your mind lately that you wish I understood better?
- If your anger had a size and a shape and a color, what would it look like?

If you think that your child has hidden concerns, you may need to speculate aloud.

- Sometimes we are angry because we are worried about something. I wonder if you are afraid that something bad might happen to you or someone else in this family?
- I wonder if you are worried that something else might happen that is bad?
- The last time you were this angry was when _____ happened. Does that still bother you? Is what's happening now a reminder of that?
- Are you worried you might have to fight in a war?
- Are you worried that people you love might die or get hurt?

Discuss vengeance.

- What would you like to see happen to the people who did this bad thing?
- In what ways is a person's anger good and helpful? In what ways can anger be bad?
- America went to war in Afghanistan to stop terrorism. What do you think about that? How does that make you feel?
- What punishment should the people who did this receive?

Discuss what to do with anger. (The "A" in SAFE stands for action steps.)

- You can talk about how you feel without hurting anybody.
- You can write out your feelings. You can draw a picture of how you feel.
- You can throw a ball against a wall.
- You can pray and ask God to help you feel better. Ask God for advice on what to do.
- You can turn your anger inside out and do something nice for someone.
- What ideas do you have?

- Anger isn't nice.
- Don't feel that way.
- I'm surprised at you.
- There is no need to feel angry.
- I wish you wouldn't say such things. You're upsetting your little sister.

Sometimes my anger over what happened shows. Is that okay for my kids to see? How can I be more even-tempered when discussing the events that happened?

Feeling anger and reporting it is fine, especially when you have experienced some kind of loss. It really depends on how you report your anger. If you are loud and frightening, or if you swear or slam doors, your anger is out of control and you are not helping your kids. Talking to a spouse, good friend, or a professional can help. If you can simply say, "I'm really angry over what happened" your children will be fine. You may want to rehearse how you can express yourself to your kids without letting your anger get the better of you.

If you say something in anger and then regret it later, tell your kids why you believe what you said was inappropriate. Let them know if you see that your anger is starting to diminish over time. "I was really angry at first but I'm feeling less angry these days. Have you noticed?"

Fear That a Parent Is in Danger

20

What if a bad guy shoots you?

—Mickey S., age 6, talking to his mother who is a police officer

Spend as much time as you can with the people you care about because you never know if you are going to see them again.

—Alicia A., age 13

Some live longer than others, so enjoy everything you can . . . Always take a loving hug . . . Just imagine the last step, or your last loving kiss. I can't bear to imagine anymore. . . .

—Lea C., age 13

Tragedies, loss, and frightening news stories can poke holes in a child's sense of security. When the world becomes a scary place, many children worry about their parents' safety. They may fear separation from them. This is especially true when a parent works at a dangerous job or is a member of the military. Kids may also worry if a parent must travel a lot on business. They miss the security of having that parent around on a daily basis.

During trying times, fear for a parent's safety is usually temporary. (See Chapter 6 for a discussion of what to say when kids are worried about their parents in the immediate aftermath of some tragedy or frightening event.) Still, it can linger for weeks. And even when the fear is lessened, new upsetting events can trigger another round of anxiety and worry. Kids are fairly helpless when it comes to influencing their parent's choice of careers. Eventually, they must learn to live with the fact that their parents cannot be protected.

During the Work Phase of trauma and loss, children may not show obvious worry for a parent's safety. Having learned that there is nothing they can do to protect a parent, they may worry beneath the surface. They may choose not to bring up their concerns. Or they may bring them up less directly:

"Can't you stay home from work today?"

"No. Why do you ask?"

"I don't know. I just want you to."

Parents need to be alert for these underlying concerns and not rely on the children to raise the issue clearly.

Since the terrorist attack on America in September 2001, children are much more aware of the dangers faced by police officers and firefighters. And many children have parents who were called into active duty in the armed forces or who were stationed in high-risk areas of the world. There are about 50,000 single parents who are called into military service. There are also about 50,000 dual-service married couples. In time of war, these 100,000 families must be split up while the parents serve their country, and relatives or friends care for the children.

If your child still speaks up about concerns for your safety (or for the safety of some other family member) after some time has passed, a brief reassuring comment will not be sufficient. Try to have a more in-depth talk before trying to ease your child's mind.

- It has been many weeks since those firefighters were killed. You still worry about me when I have to go to work (as a police officer, firefighter, and so on). What kinds of things do you worry about?

- It's normal to have some worries. Do you ever notice that they go away sometimes or are you always worried and concerned?

- When you worry about me, what kinds of things do you tell yourself that make you feel better?

- Are there things you want me to do when I'm working that would make you believe I'm less likely to get hurt?

- I'm glad you mentioned this. I don't always know how you are feeling unless you tell me.

- Do you and your friends ever talk about this? What do they say?

- If a friend of yours was worried that his (her) mother or father might get hurt or killed while doing their job, what kinds of things would you say to your friend?

    If your child had shown strong fears initially about your safety but seemed to overcome those fears, it's okay to bring up the topic weeks or months later. You won't reawaken those fears by doing that. And if your child is still concerned, you've given him or her an opportunity to talk.

- After the World Trade Center collapsed you were worried that I might get hurt or killed. You don't seem so worried anymore. Do I have that right?

- It's not unusual to still have some worries even though everything has turned out okay for us. Do you still worry sometimes that I might get hurt in my job?

- It has been a while since we last talked about how you worry about me when I'm at work. Do you still worry about that? Do you worry less or more than you did before? Why do you think it has changed?

    Give reassurances that make sense. If your child is very aware that your job is dangerous, don't pretend it is not. Emphasize steps you have taken to insure your safety.

- You're right. Being a police officer can be dangerous. But I am very well trained and I do my best to make sure I'll be safe. Most police officers never get seriously hurt.

- I suppose I would worry about you, too, if you ever grew up to be a firefighter. But I would tell myself that you are well trained and that you are not taking unnecessary risks.

- I wonder if there is something else you'd like me to do that would make you think I was safer in my job?

- Yes, my job can be dangerous. But everybody on the job looks out for each other. We can always count on each other for help if it is needed.

- I'll be fine. (Too dismissive and vague. Your child's fears won't be put to rest this easily. Start a conversation, don't put an end to it.)

- I thought we already went over this. (Don't criticize your child for having concerns. He or she will learn to avoid bringing the topic up.)

- You worry too much. (Perhaps. But maybe your child worries because your comments have not had a calming effect.)

- Yes, I could get killed. That's what happens sometimes to people with my job. (A bit blunt. Follow this up with statements on how you take care to protect yourself. Emphasize that you will be okay—which is very likely.)

When it comes to easing my children's minds, my husband and I have differing views. I like to give reassurances whenever possible. He says that the kids need to learn that life is hard and that bad things sometimes happen. He says that reassurances give children the false idea that life can always be wonderful. Who is right?

Young children, especially under age five or six, need to trust that the world is safe and predictable. Parents should give them reassurances that are strong and clear. Don't mention life's uncertainties simply in the name of honesty (*"Yes dear, there might be another school shooting. You can't prevent them all."*) Younger children put things into black-white terms. Either the world is safe or it is not. Give them the message it is safe. If their world is not safe (violence in the neighborhood or school) let them know what's being done to bring about safety. Let them know you will do everything you can to protect them.

Older kids do understand that safety and security is not guaranteed. They need reassurances that the adults are taking steps to bring about safety even though some people might get hurt. You cannot guarantee an outcome (personal safety) but you can guarantee that people in power are doing what they can to maximize safety.

Yes, children eventually will realize that the world can be dangerous at times. But what is more important for them to learn is that danger can be minimized or that resources are available to help when someone is in danger. In other words, children need to develop a sense that something can be done in the face of danger. That sense of optimism is nourished when kids know they can talk to their parents about their worries and concerns.

What to Say to Kids When a Parent Can't Cope Well

21

A youth was questioning a lonely old man.
"What is life's heaviest burden?" he asked.
And the old fellow answered sadly, "To have nothing to carry."

—Anonymous

Jill didn't know whether she was lucky or unlucky this past year. In January, she awoke in the middle of a wintry night to the smell of smoke. Her family escaped the house fire—her three kids suffered minor smoke inhalation but their lives were spared. In June, her husband suffered a serious head injury in a car accident. He is slowly recovering. In September, she heard from an old friend and former neighbor who revealed that her eighteen-year-old son committed suicide a few weeks after starting college. Jill knew the boy. She had been his babysitter many nights. He had been such a happy child. What could have gone so wrong? And of course, news of the terrorist attacks on America only added to her gloom.

As Thanksgiving approached, Jill was still feeling blue. She took no pleasure in the holiday season. She always felt exhausted. Her husband was on his way to full health but the months of treatment had made her the primary parent. The house fire had left them homeless for months—they had to live with relatives and friends while their home was being rebuilt. The children had fared pretty well considering how scary the year had been for them. Yes, at times they seemed unnecessarily demanding. They fought with each other over small things—something Jill had no patience for what-

142

soever. There was no family summer vacation to speak of. When she wasn't at work or cleaning house or looking after the kids she was looking after her husband.

Right before Thanksgiving she overheard her mother giving the children a stern lecture. Couldn't the children see that their mother was stressed and tired? Couldn't they try harder to clean their rooms and stop their squabbling? Couldn't they think of their parents' needs instead of their own?

Jill knew that her mom had a point. But she also knew that it hadn't been an easy year on the kids, either. She felt guilty for being less available to them the past few months. She had spoken to them about their own fears, especially when their dad was in the hospital. But she hadn't been able to devote herself to them, as she would have liked. Now the holidays were near and she knew she wouldn't be up to par no matter how hard she tried. How should she approach the children about all this?

When Depression or Fear Overwhelm Parents

When the rug is pulled out from under us it can be difficult to pick ourselves up, dust ourselves off, and march forward. Tragedy and loss can overwhelm even hardy people. It is not a sign of emotional weakness to be overwhelmed. The sudden and unexpected death of a loved one, for example, can temporarily turn a person's life completely upside down. Horrendous, senseless violence against a family member can shake us to our core. In a flash, couples can suddenly become single parents. Kids become motherless or fatherless. Overnight, the world can seem cold, unloving, and dangerous. Plodding forward is very hard then. Loving support from others is crucial but it doesn't quickly heal us. Healing takes time. During that time we may not be at our best.

When you aren't coping well, you probably need someone to talk to regularly. A friend may be just fine, or seeking a professional might be wise. You may need to see your physician if you can't sleep or if you aren't eating. And you may need to speak to your kids about how you are doing—not to overwhelm them, but simply to make it clear what they can expect. They are probably worried about you, too.

Parents who are struggling to cope during difficult or scary times may make one of two mistakes. Not wanting to be a burden, they act as if nothing is really wrong and don't talk about their feelings with their children. But the kids usually sense that something is wrong and they are left feeling confused or concerned. At the other extreme, some parents reveal too much about their feelings and the children feel more scared and helpless.

The SAFE approach comes in handy here. **In particular, giving kids achievable tasks (the "A" in SAFE stands for Action) that will help make your day go easier, can help your children feel less helpless. You must also ease their minds and acknowledge their concerns. Don't pretend all is well when it is not, but assure them that all will get better and that any current problems are temporary.**

- It must be hard for you when you see that I am tense and impatient.
- I can see it worries you that I am not as happy as I'd like to be.
- Do you ever worry about me? What kinds of worries about me do you have?
- I snapped at you and I shouldn't have. I'm just feeling tired and worn out. Thanks for trying to understand.
- You are such a big help to me when you _____.
- Later today I need you to clean your room (rake leaves, and so on). I'm sure you'd rather play but it helps me so much when you help out. I'll remind you later on.
- I've been very stressed out and I'm sure you've noticed I get mad easily. I want you to know that I'm starting to feel a little better and I know I'll be feeling a lot better soon.
- I am feeling stressed but I know it's only temporary. I won't always feel this way.
- Even though I'm feeling sad and worried, I have many things I feel happy about and grateful for. Let me tell you what some of them are.
- When I feel bad I say some prayers (talk to Grandma, call a friend, play a game with you, and so on). That often makes me feel a little better.

- I can't handle this anymore.
- I'm going crazy.
- When will I ever be happy again?
- Nothing feels good anymore.

- You're not making things any easier for me. (*Better:* It's so helpful when you _____.)
- I hate life.
- Life will never be the same again.
- Don't you care about how I feel? (Younger kids have a hard time putting themselves in your shoes. Older kids can empathize somewhat but still are just kids. *Better:* I'm doing the best I can right now. It will help me a lot if you would _____.)
- Just leave me alone.
- Everything is fine. (*Better:* I wish things were better but they will be soon. Right now I'm feeling a little tired and upset. I won't always feel that way.)
- Don't worry about me. Mind your own business. (If your kids are worried, that comment won't reassure them. *Better:* Thanks for your concern. You are right. I haven't been very happy for some time. But I'm feeling a little better every day.)

If you are irritable and impatient with the children, apologize without being dramatic or giving a long list of reasons why you are stressed.

- I'm sorry. I shouldn't have spoken to you like that.
- I was wrong to have said that. What I meant to say was _____.
- I'm being difficult right now. Sorry. I've got a lot on my mind.
- I was a little gruff with you earlier today. I'm sorry about that. You didn't deserve it.

Don't Say:

- I wouldn't have to speak like this to you if you'd only _____.
- Well what do you expect me to say? I wouldn't be so crabby if you'd learn to _____.
- I'm so sorry. I'm just so worried. I'm not sleeping well, I cry a lot. Nobody is helping me. I feel so alone. . . .

Sometimes one parent is coping better than the other is. Or perhaps a grandparent is called upon to help when a parent is struggling with loss or anxiety. At such times, the person who is less overwhelmed must answer the children's questions or give reassurances to them that the other adult will feel better.

Say:

- You seem worried about Mom. She is feeling sad because _____. She is starting to feel a little better each day.

- I'm here to help out Mom and Dad until they feel better. It's nice to have this extra time with you.

- You kids have been very helpful, especially when you _____.

- I bet you'll be glad when Mom and Dad are feeling better.

Don't Say:

- Don't bother Daddy. (*Better:* Daddy is resting now. Is there something I can help you with?)

- Can't you see that Mommy is tired and doesn't want to be disturbed? (It is a good idea to get feedback from the other parent on what she can or cannot do. Being overprotective can make a person feel even worse. Better to ask that person, "If the kids come to you to play [help with homework, drive them somewhere, and so on] do you want me to play with them instead or do you want to do it?")

- Can't you kids behave? Don't you care how your mom and dad are feeling?

- You're making your dad feel even worse.

When a parent really is feeling overwhelmed, it can be hard to do and say the right things. It takes energy to think before one speaks or to spend time with the kids doing some fun activity. When you are very stressed you don't have a lot of energy. All you want to do is rest or get away from the daily hassles. Any suggestions?

Parents who are feeling overwhelmed by tragedy or loss don't have many energy reserves. The daily chores of life can become quite taxing. These parents often make their situation worse by berating themselves for not being upbeat or not giving their kids quality time. Ironically, they spend much energy putting themselves down—which depletes their energy reserves and makes it harder for them to be as available to their children—which causes more self-criticism. When they do try to spend time with their kids—playing games or assisting with homework—they are often preoccupied and not fully present. Then they feel bad about *that*.

These parents need to find a comfortable zone where they can lower their high expectations of themselves but still not give in to depression. If they want to spend some playtime with the kids, they should do so in way that is manageable. Try to be fully present during that time. They should force themselves to smile more in their children's presence. The act of smiling can make us feel happier. If it is a struggle to say the right words, or if a parent fears he or she may snap at the kids the next time they are overheard arguing, it is a good idea to plan ahead. Review what can be said to the kids when they act in predictable ways. What can be said the next time that the kids are squabbling? The next time they don't turn off the TV when asked? The next time they whine that they want something?

Quality couple time may be lacking in stressed homes. A couple who sits together for fifteen minutes a night and simply chitchats or gives one another a back rub can do a lot to build up depleted energy reserves. (Read my book *How to Say It: For Couples* for many suggestions on how couples can cope during difficult times.) Single parents need some other adult they can talk to or who can help out occasionally. Social support is a huge help during trying times.

When There Are New Warnings of More Terrorism

22

I've heard on the radio and TV, the only way to beat hate is with love. Our country will win in the end because we have hearts of gold, not ones of stone.

—Shivani S., age 13

Kelley put her books in her book bag and was almost ready to walk to the bus stop. She glanced at the television. Her mom was watching the morning news. Commentators were discussing the latest governmental warning that a terrorist attack on America could happen within three days. Americans were supposed to go about their business yet remain on alert.

"I'm ready to go," Kelley said.

Her mom turned off the TV and accompanied her daughter to the bus stop. Was Kelley worried about what she heard? She didn't say anything to her mom about it if she was. Should her mom say anything? Or maybe Kelley really wasn't paying attention after all. . . .

Jared and Jennifer are of elementary school age and live in Oklahoma City. Their mom works in a government building. When terrorists struck the Pentagon and the World Trade Center in September 2001, Oklahoma City went on high alert. Caution dictated that any city or building that might possibly be a target of terrorism should be protected. As it turned out, Oklahoma City was not the target of terrorism that day. But the people of the city had to respond defensively and many children were worried.

If a school shooting occurs, schools in the surrounding area and even schools far away are put on alert. Students once regarded school bomb threats as pranks and not serious threats. These days, bomb threats leave students, teachers, and parents worried and on edge.

Terrorists have not destroyed the American way of life. They haven't even come close. But they have succeeded in making us all look over our shoulders once in a while.

If you don't want to alarm your children about recent terrorist threats and you believe it is very likely that your child has not heard about recent warnings of possible terrorist strikes, you can ask more general questions.

- It's been a while since we talked about what's been happening in the world (the school shootings, the terrorist attacks, and so on). What have you been thinking lately?
- Do any of your friends ever talk about terrorism?
- Does anything still worry you about what's been happening in the world?
- What's been worrying you lately?

If you know that your child has heard about the warnings, say:

- What do you think about that?
- Does this make you worried?
- It makes everyone a little nervous when they hear such reports. Still, the last time a warning was given nothing happened.
- I'm not that worried. I don't like hearing that news but it won't change anything I do.
- Terrorists like to make us afraid. They like thinking that some people will worry about more attacks, even if no attacks are going to happen.
- The last time we had a warning nothing happened.
- Our government and police have better ways of protecting us now.

- The world is so frightening.
- Maybe we should all stay home for the next few days until the warning passes.

- You must be so scared by all this. (Not necessarily. If you are over-protective you may scare your child, or you may smother him and cause him to pull away and not want to talk with you about these events.)
- I'm glad I'm not your age. We've created a terrible world for you and kids your age to live in.
- By the time you grow up the world will be in a terrible mess. There may not even be a world.

If your child is not concerned, say:

- I'm glad. I don't think it is something you need to worry about. But if you do get concerned, please let me know and we'll discuss it.
- That's good to hear. Why do you feel that way?
- What kind of warning would make you worried? (This is an opportunity to respond to hidden concerns your child might have.)

If your child says:

Is something bad going to happen?

Say: I'm not worried that something will happen to us. Yes, something might happen but probably not. Our government is more prepared than before.

Don't Say: Let's hope not.; Maybe.; Absolutely not.; Don't worry about it. (All of these responses are incomplete. They may add to anxiety because they are not reassuring or they close off communication.)

When will they get the terrorists?

Say: They have captured many of them. It will take a long time to get all of them. But the ones that they have not found don't have money to do all the bad things they want to do.

Don't Say: It's impossible to get all of them. There will always be terrorists. (Offer more hope that the world is nevertheless safer from terrorism than it was before the war against terrorism.)

Let's stay home and not go to school (work).

Say: You sound worried. What worries you? I can see why you might feel worried but I wouldn't go to work or let you go to school if I thought we were in danger.

Don't Say: That's being silly. . . . You're letting your imagination go wild. Everyone else will be going to school, you'll be the only one who is afraid.

The war on terrorism is bound to go on for years. In the meantime, the United States could be a victim again of some attack. There may also be a war in Iraq or in the Middle East. It seems that the news will be scary for some time to come. What impact will this have on our children? What is the effect of not being able to completely enjoy life? Do kids just ignore the news after a while or will it adversely affect them?

It is not what happens to us that dictates how we will ultimately be affected. It is our response to adversity. The same adverse event can affect different people in different ways, depending largely upon the resources available to help them cope. On average, a child with a strong, loving home life, and parents who can keep the lines of communication open, will cope better than a child with far less emotional support. No one wants to see people we love suffer through loss and tragedy. And yet for many of us, it is only through anxiety and pain that we develop a sense of hardiness—a sense that we have what it takes to get through difficult times. Adversity also has the potential of strengthening our religious beliefs if we are willing—not to turn from God in anger, wondering why he allows such awful things to happen—but to turn to him in need and trust that he is with us and cares about our ultimate good.

As a parent, you can instill strong values in your children during difficult times. They will watch you to see how you handle the upsetting events and they will learn from you. If you listen carefully to your children and respond to them with sincerity and a dash of optimism, (and if you are always available to them), they will probably fare well no matter what happens.

When Holidays Approach After Tragedy Strikes

23

Can I fly up to him on Christmas?

—Kyle T., age 5, asking his mom if he can see his dad in heaven

Little by little, but not every day, hope nudges forward in the hearts of people grieving a loss or bearing an unfair burden. Some days hope may only be the small smile that they briefly show; or it appears as the grin on their children's faces as they open a birthday present. But hope competes with other, powerful feelings during troubling times. Especially when a person or family has suffered a loss, grief and anger can overtake any of the more uplifting emotions.

The holiday season can be a difficult time for many families grieving a loss. Birthdays and anniversaries also are painful, at least during the first years. It takes time for good memories to bring smiles of joy and gratitude instead of tears. An anniversary date of some loss or trauma also evokes strong emotions.

"If I hear one more Christmas song . . ." a man once said to me as his father lay dying in a hospital bed. It was a tough time of year for him as warm memories of the past collided with the harsh realities of the present. *"It's so hard to see everybody else shopping for gifts as if life is just the same as it always was. I watch the shoppers get aggravated over such small things. Don't they understand what can be taken from them without warning?"*

For some people, holidays are hard times. For others, the holidays are a diversion from the worries of life. When the world becomes a scary place, when troubling times make us uneasy or scared, or when loved ones have died, talking to kids about how they are doing—especially during a holiday season or anniversary—can be helpful.

If your child seems fairly unaffected by world or local events, the holiday time can be an opportunity for your child to consider the plight of others.

- What do you think this holiday is like for the families of those who were killed?

- Let's say a prayer for those people who are sad during the holidays.

- Is there someone in your school who might be kind of sad at Christmas (Hanukkah)? I wonder if there is something you could say or do that might make them feel a little better?

- This is the first holiday Mrs. Smith will spend without her husband. Any ideas on what we could do that might help her?

- Soon it will be the anniversary of the terrorist attack (shooting, bombing, and so forth). Do you ever think about what happened? How do you think the families are doing?

- If someone you loved was killed a year ago, what would you want to happen on the anniversary of the death? What things would help make it special?

If some loss or tragedy personally affected your child, first try to understand your child's perspective without trying to automatically change it. If you want your child to feel better, keep in mind that it is normal to have a mixture of feelings on holidays or anniversaries and that people often feel a little better when someone listens and understands.

- It's sad without _____ being here with us, isn't it?

- Do you ever feel okay for a while and then feel kind of sad?

- In some ways this holiday feels like ones from the past, but in other ways it feels very different.

- I wish _____ were here, too.

- What feels okay about this holiday? What feels the worst?

- Even though we are sad that _____ isn't with us, it's nice when we can also feel glad about some things.

- Is there something about the way you feel that you would like me to understand?

- Sometimes I can guess at how you must be feeling, but sometimes I need you to tell me.

- I'd like to hear what you have to say about today and what it means to you. Anything you say is important to me.

     Getting through a holiday or anniversary helps you and your family to accept the reality of what happened. **Discuss ways that the day (or season) can be spent that will move the family toward healing. It is important to get input from all family members and to treat comments with respect.**

- It's okay if you have some fun or feel good this holiday. It isn't necessary to feel sad all the time. What are your thoughts?

- I'd like to spend part of the time doing something special.

- If you could do three special things on that day what would they be?

- This is going to be a sad holiday for many people. I wonder if there is anything that we could do for some of them?

- Let's make sure we spend a little time on Hanukkah (Christmas, someone's birthday) remembering _____ and his life. (Rituals can be very helpful. Say a prayer together, plant some flowers, sing a song, attach an "I love you" note to a helium balloon and send it flying . . .)

- Try not to think about it today. You think about it enough on other days.

- Holidays will never be enjoyable anymore. (*Better:* I'm very sad right now. But I'll feel better eventually. I just wish some things hadn't happened . . .)

- If Daddy were here with us he'd want you to feel happy. (*Better:* Daddy loves you and knows how you feel. He also knows that one day you won't feel so sad. It will be nice when we can all feel happier again.)

- It's just another day. It doesn't mean any more than any other day. (*Better:* Even when we seem to be feeling happier, some days can bring back memories that make us a little sad. Some memories can be sweet, too.)

- If you can't be in a good mood today then maybe you should go to another room. (*Better:* You don't seem to be in a good mood today. I wonder if you are thinking about _____? It's normal for your feelings to be a lot stronger on a day like today.)

     If your child says:
     I don't care if it's my birthday. I miss Mommy and she's not here!
     Say: I miss her, too. It can be hard sometimes to feel good when someone you love can't be with you.

I know how you feel. She was with you on your last birthday and you're sad and angry that she's not here now.

I'm very happy it is your birthday. I'm also very sad that Mommy isn't here. I feel both of those feelings.

Don't Say:

We are all trying to have a nice day and you're ruining it. Can't you just try to have some fun?

Your brothers and sisters aren't acting this way. Why are you? Mommy would be upset if she knew you had this attitude.

My stomach hurts when I think about _____.

Say:

That probably means you are sad. I'm sad, too.

What exactly are you thinking when you think about _____?

Sometimes our emotions—our feelings—show up as aches and pains in our bodies. If your stomach could talk, what would it say?

Don't Say:

Try not to think about it.

Your stomach always hurts. The hurt will go away.

Just ignore it.

I'm not looking forward to Christmas (vacation, visiting relatives, or some other previously enjoyable activity).

Say:

Tell me more about that.

Something about Christmas bothers you right now. What is it?

In what ways will Christmas be different for you this year? Could something happen that would make it a little better?

Don't Say:

You'll feel better once it happens.

Don't upset everyone else. We're trying to enjoy it.

Why do you focus on the bad feelings? . . . It's only as bad as you make it . . . Why must you always say things like that?

My teenage son was killed during a robbery while working at a convenience store. His younger siblings miss him terribly. How can we make the upcoming holidays less sad? My fear is that no holiday will ever be happy again. I want my kids to have fun and not feel so bad. I don't know the best way to handle it.

There are layers to your grief and your children's grief. One layer is the pain of missing your son and of not having him physically near. Another layer is the thoughts you have about how he died. Tragic, unexpected, and violent death is usually much harder to cope with than the death that is peaceful and expected. Another layer might be unresolved feelings the survivors have. For example, one of your children might feel guilty about having argued with your son one day. Still another layer might be the anxieties your kids have that the world is a frightening place. They might be worried about your safety or how you are coping.

That is why "cheering up" someone can be complicated. The layers of grief and pain might be so numerous that anything you do to help only scratches the surface of what's really bothering them.

However, children often grieve in sporadic episodes. One minute they are sad, the next they are playing and laughing. Don't be surprised if that is what happens with your children. They will also be taking their cue from you. Make sure you try to do something pleasurable—something that will make you laugh, if possible. Give them permission to have fun. Acknowledge any feelings of grief they have, let them know that such feelings are normal, remind them that people can and do feel better over time. Talk about the loved one often but try not to always sound despairing. It's normal for feelings to be bittersweet—sad, but laced with joy and gratitude for what you had. Let your kids know that you feel both ends of the emotional spectrum and all of the emotions in between.

Sometimes, a family feels guilty for enjoying themselves at a holiday gathering after a loved one has died. It can help to set sometime aside for everyone to remember that person. Perhaps some stories can be told. Then move on to other activities. That way, there is room for all emotions to have their say.

Finally, there are many people—some you don't even know—who are thinking about you and praying for you during this time. Remember that. You are not as alone as you sometimes feel.

Part
Four

The Well-Being Phase of Trauma, Tragedy, or Terror

When tragedy or loss uproots your life, your whole purpose and the meaning to your existence can flip upside down. You used to have specific reasons to get up every morning. Life made sense. Then in one swift movement everything changed. To make it even harder, you were then expected to put everything back together again when important pieces were missing. Not only have some people perhaps gone from your life, your own values about what is important may have stood up and handed in their resignation, leaving you without a clear sense of where to go, how to act, and what to believe in.

"I'm afraid," people say in the Worry Phase, the first phase after loss or tragedy. "I can't believe this is happening. Please God, don't let this be happening."

"I'm lost," people say in the Work Phase. "I get through the day but nothing feels quite the same. Though, some days are better than others."

"I have hope," people say in the Well-Being Phase. "And I am grateful for what was good."

Perhaps the most common mistake adults make when talking to kids about difficult times is presuming that the children are automatically resilient and that they will move quickly to the Well-Being Phase. A few days after the World Trade Center crumbled, parents watched their kids play and do homework and assumed they were not that affected. But many children were affected. Parents *want* to believe that their children are handling things well so they sometimes see what they want to see. The only way to know the extent your child is affected is to watch, ask questions, and be willing to chat about it again later on.

The Well-Being Phase overlaps a bit with the other two phases. Even when a person's life is back on track, remnants of the other phases show up now and then. To experience moments of deep sadness or anxiety even years after suffering a loss means that the loss was profound or that aspects of the event are still unresolved. However, feelings of well-being may still predominate.

The Key Elements of the Well-Being Phase

If a cherished loved one dies you will always miss that person. If you experienced a traumatic event in your life the memory of it will probably not go away, though it might fade. Painful memories and the feelings associated with grief are normal. They don't necessarily indicate a lack of well-being.

There are key elements that show up when a person experiences well-being, despite whatever tragedy has befallen him or her.

A feeling of being lovable: Knowing one is loved and lovable helps sooth pain and promotes healing. Children need to be reminded and shown that they are loved during trying times.

A feeling of gratitude: Someone with peace of mind and well-being is able to focus on the wonderfulness of what was and what can be, instead of emphasizing the unfairness of what was lost. Memories bring a smile instead of pain. The small things in life are seen as riches to be treasured. Parents can talk to their kids about what they are grateful for during difficult times. Knowing that their parents can still feel some gratitude instills a sense of peace in children and nurtures their optimism.

A lessening of fear and an optimistic sense of being able to cope with what life hands out: It isn't enough to be out of danger. A person must feel that he or she has resources to handle what life can dish out. Those resources can also include such things as reliance on other people or faith in God. Children need to know that their parents are available to them. They need to realize that whatever pain they feel can lessen and that they can act in ways to make life happy again.

A feeling that life still has meaning and purpose: Without a sense of purpose we feel lost, depressed, and uncertain. Children may not develop a philosophical approach to life but they do have goals—learning to ride a two-wheeler, making the football team, getting a driver's license, getting accepted into a certain college—and parents can help children cope by fostering and encouraging important goals.

Joy and grief, pain and purpose, peace of mind and uncertainty—these things often coexist. Sometimes, the art of well-being involves understanding and accepting that paradox.

24

Talking about Heroism—and the Hero Inside Your Child

No they didn't die scared
They didn't die wrong
They stood up for America
And were incredibly strong

—Amy B., age 14, writing about the heroes of 9/11

Tragedy and loss make us look down in grief. Heroes make us look up. Tragedy makes us ask, "Why, God?" Heroes make us ask, "How can I help, God?" Tragedy tries to crush a spirit that heroes uplift.

Chris Haney, age 11, climbed forty feet up a pine tree to rescue a girl who was dangling there after having been shocked by a power line.

Chris Wright, a seventh grader, dragged his father from a river after the man suffered an epileptic fit, hoisted him into the pickup truck, and drove him to safety.

Amanda Valence, 14, grabbed her friend Edna, who had just been attacked by an alligator, and maneuvered her fifty yards to shore while the alligator tried to close the gap. Edna would have surely died without Amanda's selfless act of courage.[1]

Children are instinctively drawn to bold acts of heroism. Perhaps it is because children feel more vulnerable and a world full of heroes is a world that feels safe. But adults are instinctively drawn to such acts, as well. Psychologist Jonathan Haidt conducts research on what he has called "elevation"—the uplifting feeling of awe that sometimes moves us to tears whenever we witness acts of moral beauty such as com-

[1]The three examples were from People magazine, December 10, 2001, pp. 88, 106.

passion, courage, and loyalty. Physical sensations, such as warmth in the chest or a tingling sensation on the head or neck, usually accompanies it. And perhaps most important of all, it motivates us to become better people ourselves.

Children develop morally as well as physically and intellectually. In one study, an adult left a room with young children and said she would return shortly. In the meantime, the children heard a crash and a child's cry from another room. Would any of the children leave their room to offer help? About one-half of five-year-olds did leave the room. But only 40 percent of fourth graders and 30 percent of sixth graders offered to help. The older children indicated they feared being punished if they left, so that was why they did not investigate the crash. If that study is any indication, then parents must teach not only obedience but also good judgment. Sometimes it might be important to break a rule in order to help another person. Kids need help making that distinction.

Another reason older kids do not always act compassionately towards another has to do with peer pressure and peer evaluation. Many kids do not want to stand out and call attention to themselves for fear of being laughed at or made fun of. Consequently, bystanders watching a bully tease a classmate may do nothing. A parent's guidance in this area can make a world of difference.

In the wake of trauma, loss, or tragedy, it can be helpful to remind our children that heroes exist. It helps them along the road to well-being by offering hope for their future and faith that, even during dark times, good can overcome evil. It is also a good idea to identify the heroes in your children's lives—the ordinary people who nevertheless make sacrifices for others in order to be living examples of love.

Watch stories with your children about rescuers, police officers, firefighters, and others who risk their lives. Discuss the stories with your kids.

- What did you think of that story?
- What do you think about someone who risks his or her own life in order to save the life of somebody else?
- Who is a hero to you? Why?
- Can a person be a hero even if they don't save another person's life?
- When I hear stories about people doing heroic things, I get a good feeling inside.

- When I hear stories of heroes, it makes me want to do something nice for others.
- When I hear stories of heroes, it makes me realize that the most important thing about life is trying to love other people.

Encourage your child to show compassion toward others. Discuss safe ways to help those in need.

- If you saw a bully teasing a classmate, how do you think the kid being teased feels?
- If you were being bullied, what would you want others to do?
- If someone really needs help, you can always look for a grown-up.
- If someone you know is sad about something, what could you do that might help?
- Sometimes in order to do the right thing you have to be willing to look foolish to some of your friends. How hard do you think that is?
- People who end up being heroes often start out by being nice to people in smaller ways. What ways could you be helpful to people?
- What things might you have done already that were courageous?

Label your child in clear, positive ways. Broad, nonspecific praise is less effective than specific comments.

- When you did that, it showed me you have compassion.
- I liked it when you said that. You are a kind person.
- You kept working on that even though it was difficult. That shows you can persevere.
- Thanks for telling the truth. You are an honest person.
- That was nice of you to share your food with your friend. That tells me you are not a selfish person and that you can be generous.

- Don't do anything dangerous. (Yes, you don't want your child taking foolish risks. Better to talk about the kinds of behaviors you would like him or her to avoid than make broad comments.)
- You have to look out for yourself. You can't count on anybody.

I worry that if I talk enthusiastically about heroism, my children may take unnecessary risks and get hurt. How do you teach children to help others while avoiding risks?

If your child develops a strong sense of compassion and justice and knows right from wrong, then he or she has probably already acted in a selfless way for another. (And you deserve congratulations for that.) There isn't a way to prevent someone who has what it takes to be a "hero" not to take risks. Risks are always part of the equation. Maybe what you can teach your child is judgment. For example, it would not be good judgment for a person who cannot swim to dive into deep water to save someone who was drowning. Fighting with bare hands against an attacker who has a weapon is poor judgment unless the fighter is very skilled. You can talk to your child about various scenarios where good judgment might be finding an adult who can be of assistance instead of trying to help out by oneself.

Heroism at its most glorious and impressive is not just luck and skill. We are uplifted when we witness or hear about such morally beautiful acts because a dimension of our soul has been tapped. For that moment we realize at a deep, heartfelt level that all human beings are connected; that we are all brothers and sisters. When you talk about heroism with your children and teach compassion, you are putting them in touch with their spiritual side as much as anything else.

Gratitude

Be thankful
Even if you are deaf, you can hear Jesus play the loving music;
Even if you are blind you can see Jesus rising;
Even if you are paralyzed you can feel the presence of Jesus in you.

—Anna C., age 10, from a Thanksgiving poem

When we are saddened by someone else's misfortune we usually count our blessings. We hold our children just a little tighter and overlook life's minor annoyances that seemed so major just a little while ago. When we hear about some tragedy, some war, some senseless, barbaric act of terrorism, we get our priorities straight and realize that we have taken life for granted and truly have much to be grateful for.

Gratitude is a healing force.

But gratitude is harder to come by when we are the victims of some untimely loss or tragedy. Instead of saying, "Thank God" we ask, "Why, God?" and believe that fate has struck us an unfair blow. In the early phase of tragedy, it is a mistake to tell victims to "look at the bright side" and to be grateful for what they have left. Those suffering from loss or misfortune are grieving what they lost. Well-intentioned advice givers often say things like "It was God's will . . . It could have been even worse . . . At least you still have your health . . . Try to be grateful for the years you had together. . . ." What they are really saying to the one suffering is "You shouldn't feel the way you do." And the other person is lonelier for it.

Still, gratitude is a necessary part of healing. And even when all is well in one's life, gratitude for life's gifts promotes a deeper sense of inner peace. It is a good idea for parents to remind children that there is much to be grateful for. And if the child had suffered a loss or was frightened by some adversity, nurturing a grateful spirit offers comfort to all.

If your child was not directly affected by tragedy but has heard about it on the news, use that event as a springboard for comments about gratitude. **Plant a seed in your child's mind and heart that too often we take life for granted and will be happier if we feel grateful for what we have.**

- What happened to those people was horrible and very sad. It reminds me that we should all be thankful for everything we have and for the people in our lives.
- Sometimes when I'm bored I try to appreciate all of the little things in life that I would miss if I could not have them. Imagine if I couldn't see the leaves change colors in the autumn because I was blind? Imagine if I couldn't hear you play your trombone because I was deaf?
- Sometimes it is nice to look around you and take notice of everything you see. Then say "Thank you" to God for creating the universe and us.
- The people in that country are starving. They would be grateful for a piece of bread. It makes me think that I should try to not get upset when little things go wrong because at least I have food and the people I love are near me.
- I'm grateful for the people that are willing to help us when we need help.
- I'm grateful that so many people are patriotic and love our country.
- What things are you grateful for? What little things would you miss if all of a sudden they weren't there?

     Give examples of small things from your childhood that you treasured and now miss. Emphasize the feeling of gratitude, not sadness.

- When I walked up the stairs in my house they would creak. I miss that sound.
- I remember how my mother would sing songs to herself when she was cleaning the house. I miss hearing that.
- I miss the smell of my father's pipe tobacco.
- I remember the sound of the oars in the water as we rowed the boat. That was a great sound.
- I miss some of my teachers. They were really very dedicated. I appreciate what they did for me.

- I really liked the smell of Christmas cookies baking.

If your child was personally affected by some tragedy, don't preach gratitude. Instead, raise the topic gently and hear what your child has to say about it. Be understanding if your child does not feel particularly grateful.

- Sometimes after people have had a very rough time in their lives, they think about things they are grateful for. Have you had a chance to think about those things?

- Do you ever think about the way things used to be and smile at the memory?

- After people we love die we usually miss them a lot and feel sad when we think about them. Then eventually we think about them and we smile because they made our lives happier. Do you ever think of them and smile and feel good?

- Sometimes when we miss someone we feel sad, but we also feel grateful that he or she was a part of our lives. Do you ever feel grateful and sad at the same time?

- This has been a very hard year. Still, is there anything you are thankful for?

- I was just thinking how so many people were helpful to us this year. I am very thankful for their help. I especially liked _____.

- Even when bad things happen to people, some good things happen, too. Can you think of anything that happened to you that was good this year?

- It's nice to hear you talk about things you are thankful for. It feels good to talk about those things doesn't it?

How Not to Say It

If your child went through some scary or tragic time, don't scold or show impatience if he or she hasn't developed a better attitude yet.

- You always focus on the negative. Can't you think about the good things in your life? (*Better:* When you talk only about the bad things that happened, I feel sad for you. I hope someday you can also think about the things you are grateful for.)

- Stop complaining.

- Grandpa (or some other deceased relative) would be upset with you if he saw you act that way.

- Your friends don't act like you do. Why can't you be like them?
- People who can't appreciate what they have will never be happy.

If your child says:

I'm still angry about what happened!

Say: I don't blame you. What happened was very bad. Still, I hope that some day when you feel you are ready you can also think about the good things in your life.

Don't Say: You should be over it by now.

Yes, I'm glad that she was part of my life but I still miss her. I don't want her to be gone.

Say: That's normal to feel that way. I miss her, too. And at the same time I also feel thankful that she was part of our lives and I'm grateful for that.

Don't Say: But she is gone. You have to accept that.

Why should I thank God for everything he has given me? He also let bad things happen.

Say: A lot of people feel that way. I suggest that you do what I am going to do: Talk to God a lot and tell him that you are mad. Then let's see how you feel in a month or two.

Don't Say: That's a terrible thing to say.

Isn't it harder to teach our children to be grateful in a society where they are often overindulged? How can a parent or grandparent teach thankfulness?

Ingratitude stems from a sense of entitlement; a feeling of being owed. Gratitude in its deeper sense is not merely a polite "Thank you." It stems from a sense of humility. Humility is not inadequacy. It is a recognition that we are imperfect, that we do not have all the answers, that others have needs that may be more pressing than our own, that as talented or attractive as we are, we are not the be-all and end-all of this world. Children have a natural self-centered tendency. They see the world from their own vantage point and have a hard time putting themselves in others' shoes. Children don't often think about their mortality. When adults contemplate their mortality they are put in touch with all they are grateful for.

As a parent you should model gratitude. Talk about life's simple pleasures and openly express thankfulness—not just for the big, exceptional gifts—but for the mundane gifts. Try not to lose your sense of wonder. Express gratitude when showing the children the stars on a dark night, the beautiful lake or ocean, the smell after a cleansing rain. Never underestimate the value of your time and presence in your children's lives. Yes, they enjoy their video games and DVD players but your presence in their lives is immensely important and something they will eventually learn to fully appreciate—though they may be adults by then.

Restoring Hope in Your Child

26

I have a dream that one day all terrorism will come to an end. We shall find a way to make peace with other countries. We will find a way... We will find a way.

—Nick G., age 13

Just imagine being a rescue worker in New York City. You have a little spark inside that keeps you hoping to find a survivor, and that spark is what keeps you working as hard as ever.

—Jeff N., age 13

Hope tells us that life can still be worthwhile and good even when we've been deeply hurt. It is a light and a warmth that draws us in. In the early stages of grief or anxiety our hope is really desperation. We plead with God or some other powerful force to take away the awful realities that face us.

It is only after we come face to face with genuine loss or profound tragedy that a more meaningful level of hope arises.

It is the kind of hope that whispers tenderly to mourners maybe a year or so after the death of a loved one;

It is the kind of hope that lonely couples caress long after a romance has withered;

It is the kind of hope that people suffering from a terminal illness softly embrace.

It is the hope that one's life can still be good and meaningful
   despite tragedy and loss.
It is the hope that joy and peace of mind are still real possibilities,
   however remote they once seemed.
It is the hope that hope still lives.[1]

You Are Not Alone

The process of healing is underway when we have hope. In the first phase of trauma or loss, hope is often wishful thinking, based upon fear and anxiety. We are worried and uncertain so we hope and pray, desperately, for some desired outcome.

By the time the Well-Being Phase appears, fear has been transcended, at least partially. There is a greater sense of peace; there is a reality that we have made it through the worst of it. There may be a lingering grief, but there is also a stirring in one's soul that life still matters even though it is very different and very difficult. Hope at this phase is based not on fear but on faith. Having gone through a difficult period we often develop a faith that God still loves us, that life is still worth living, and that resources are available to us when we need them—that we are not alone. Hope provides us with a response to the many "What if?" questions that fear always asks:

What if we die?

What if it happens again?

What if we aren't so lucky next time?

What if our whole life changes and we're never happy?

And how does hope respond? Not with hasty, glib reassurances. Hope says:

All problems, however difficult to bear, are temporary.

That even permanent loss, such as the death of a loved one, need not bring about permanent, negative effects.

That today holds out promise for at least some degree of happiness.

Life is good even though it can be sorrowful.

You can make a difference in the life of someone you haven't even met yet—your life still matters even when you don't see any purpose to it.

[1]Paul Coleman. *Life's Parachutes: How to Land on Your Feet During Trying Times.* New York: Dell, 1993, p. 226.

God has a plan for your life that is for the good. As long as you are alive that plan is not yet completed.

As you can see, fear always looks at what might possibly go wrong. Hope looks at what can go right. Fear looks at death. Hope looks at life. Fear agitates us. Hope comforts us. Fear says "Why bother?" Hope answers "Because you cannot possibly see the big picture from your perspective. There is more to your life than you know."

Parents and caretakers have a remarkable role to play in the lives of children when life has become painful and difficult. They can, by their words and actions, show that all is not lost and thereby restore hope.

Teach children that their outlook—optimistic or pessimistic—makes a huge difference in how they handle life's ups and downs.

- I like what you just said. It was very hopeful. You are an optimist—someone who tries to find the good in things.

- If you were playing a game and believed you had no chance of winning would you still try very hard? Would you try harder if you thought you had a better chance of winning? Most people who are hopeful try harder and don't give up so quickly.

- Can you think of a time when you were very hopeful about something so you did not give up?

- Can you think of a time when you felt hopeless about something and gave up trying?

- If you keep trying you will succeed at something.

  State that the future can still be a happy one. Your kids depend on you to put matters into perspective.

- No matter what happens, I know you can feel happy again.

- Many things happen in life. Some make us sad, some happy. We will feel happy again some day.

- I will always miss your mom (a loved one who has died). I won't be happy like I was when she was here with us but I can be happy in other ways. One way I will be happy is when I remember her and I remember how she loved us.

- Bad times never last forever.

- Even when the times are rough, there will be many days when we will feel pretty good.
- If it doesn't work out the way we want we will find a way to manage.
- Somehow we will land on our feet again.
- I don't know how it will exactly happen, but I do believe things will turn out okay eventually.
- I don't know why this bad thing happened. All I know is that we are together and are meant to love and care for one another during this hard time.
- Some things in our lives have changed a lot. But the most important things have not changed—our love for one another and our belief that God cares about what we are going through.
- Even when we feel sad we can still find things that we are happy about and grateful for.
- The worst feeling is hopelessness. I don't feel that way. I feel hopeful even though I am also somewhat scared (sad, worried, angry, and so on).

In order to instill hope, your child must first feel understood. That means you must be willing to listen to concerns and empathize before you speak of hope. **You need not give profound answers to your child's questions. Simply respond in a manner that shows you understand. That can be comforting and promote hope in your child.**

- I don't blame you for feeling that way.
- I feel that way, too, sometimes.
- It's hard to feel hopeful when things are so different.
- It's hard to trust that the world is basically a good place when bad things happen.
- It is understandable you would question your faith in God.
- Anybody would be somewhat scared and worried. And yet people can be hopeful, too.
- Tell me more about that. It seems to really matter to you.
- What else do you feel?
- What is the hardest thing about being hopeful right now?
- What is easier to hope for?
- What is one thing that you wish you were more hopeful about?
- Is there something you weren't hopeful about before but now you are?
- Did you ever notice that feelings of hope can sometimes fade in and out?

The biggest mistake is expressing optimism in a glib manner or automatically dismissing a child's worries as wrong or silly. A child who doesn't feel listened to or understood will take little comfort in your optimistic words.

- Everything will be fine. (This is appropriate for a preschool child who may not be interested in the details. As kids age they need more information.)

- I'm happy. Why aren't you?

- Don't be so gloomy.

- Oh, you always think the worst.

- Everything is okay. Can't you see that?

- Stop worrying. There's nothing at all to be concerned about.

- Don't get your hopes up. (*Better:* That's a good thing to hope for. I'm also hoping that if you don't get what you want, that you will eventually be okay.)

- We will never be happy again.

- We didn't get what we wanted. I'll never believe in prayer again.

- It's useless to hope. Things will either work out or they won't. Hoping doesn't make a difference. (True, a certain outcome that is hoped for may not happen. But then you need to hope that you can handle that outcome. You need to have hope that life can still be worthwhile despite loss or injustice or tragedy.)

Can children be taught to have an optimistic outlook?

Yes. Research indicates that it is not adversity per se that is the critical element in what happens to us, but our response to adversity. And how we respond depends in large part upon our beliefs about what has happened and what might happen in the future. If you believe that you have what it takes to get through some crisis then you will persevere despite hardship and fatigue. If you don't believe that then you will give up the fight.

Parents, grandparents, and other caretakers can keep that in mind when talking to children. Find out what a child believes. If his or her outlook is pessimistic, help the child to correct any mistaken beliefs and look at the situation more positively. When the child is working on a task, praise the child's *effort* even if the outcome is not a success. Kids who are praised for their effort tend to persist at harder tasks and are therefore more likely to eventually succeed. Kids who don't persist always fail at the task at hand.

Simply telling a child "You can do it!" sounds nice but is insufficient. Remind the child of the very specific skills he or she possesses that will help bring about success. *"You know how to reread the material and find the answer . . . You know how to use a calculator . . . When you are patient and take your time you usually get it right . . . When you practice you get really good at this. . . ."*

An optimistic outlook is not just about oneself and one's skills, but about the world and the future of the world. You can explain how there have always been wars and yet there has been peace, too. You can talk about times in your life when things did not go well and yet you somehow made it through. You can point out how bad times are temporary. You can talk about the wonderful display of charity that people show when people are in need. And by all means, discuss your religious views if they help you to remain optimistic.

Making Progress Checks

27

There are no limits to the truth you can know,
To the life you can live,
To the love you can enjoy,
And to the beauty you can experience.

—Fulton J. Sheen, *bishop, author, and one of the most celebrated churchmen of the past century*

When a child suffers a physical trauma or injury, parents not only make sure that medical help is provided but also they inquire how the child is feeling even long after the incident is over. "Does your leg still feel okay?" a parent might ask six months after the cast has come off. Parents do that to make sure that everything is fine and no hidden problems are lurking.

But when a child has experienced some kind of emotional loss or trauma many parents are reluctant to probe for underlying problems long after the incident occurred. *"I don't want to make him upset . . . I don't want to rock the boat . . . She's fine now so why should I disturb her by bringing up bad memories?"* That is the faulty logic many parents use.

If a child really is doing fine, then bringing up the subject will not cause damage. If the child has unresolved issues, then raising the topic might uncover them and allow them to be discussed. Even if your child seemed unaffected by frightening world or local events, revisiting the subject when everything seems fine might reveal important information. It never hurts to ask.

- What have you learned from all that has happened?
- What was your biggest concern before? What is it today?
- What worries did you have at first that you no longer have?
- Is there anything that didn't worry you at first but that worry you now?
- Are you more or less hopeful about the future than you were before?
- Is there anything we did as a family during the crisis that you wish we had done differently?
- If it happened again, how would you react this time?
- What has made you the happiest since it happened?
- What worry or fear do you still have, even a little bit?
- Was there anything I said or did that helped the most?
- If you could give advice to some other child who has the same worries you had, what would you say?
- Has any good come out of what happened?
- What did you learn about people in general that you would not have known had this event not happened?
- Has it changed what you imagine your future to be?
- What has been the hardest thing for you in the past year?
- What surprised you the most about the past year?
- If someday your grandchildren ask you about what happened, what will be the most important thing you will tell them?

- Let's put it all behind us.
- There's no need to bring that up anymore.
- I thought you were over that. Why are you still thinking about it?

Developing a Healing Theory

Psychologist Charles Figley has worked extensively with traumatized families. He recommends that families develop a "healing theory" to put into perspective what happened, why it happened, and whether or not the family was able to manage the rough times. The healing theory should not be something they develop right away but should emerge over time after each family member has had ample opportunity to adjust to the loss or the trauma. A healing theory should ultimately have a positive emphasis. Negative explanations for tragedy such as "God doesn't love us" or "We must have been very bad for this to have happened" are not helpful. In order to develop a healing theory, there must be room for all members to freely express themselves. Anger or despair may be part of those early discussions, which is why a healing theory takes time to put into place. A healing theory tries to empower a family—to make them feel that they have some influence over what happens in their lives as they respond to adversity. Therefore, the theory emphasizes virtues such as faith, optimism, love, courage, and forgiveness. Most of all, it should "make sense" to each family member. Some family members may not fully agree with the theory but ideally all will find it to be an acceptable "first draft" until a better theory is developed.

Discuss each member's theory about why bad things happen. Try (over time, not hastily) to create the family's version of a healing theory. Younger children may have less to say but can be included in these discussions.

- We can never know for sure why some bad things happen. We can only try to make the best of it when tragedy strikes. How have we made the best of it?
- What are some positive things about the way we handled this situation?
- What are some positive things about the way our country has handled this situation? What does that say about the people of our country?
- What is something we could do as a family that would make you feel a little bit better about what happened?
- Sometimes bad things happen to people because they are in the wrong place at the wrong time. If that happens, how can people feel better about their life?

If someone in the family is angry or otherwise has a negative outlook, don't dismiss his or her concerns. Instead, say:

- I can't blame you for feeling that way. I felt that way, too. But I'm hoping there is something positive you will one day be able to say about all of this.
- You have a right to feel that way.
- A lot of people might have the same ideas you have.

- Even though what you are saying sounds gloomy and pessimistic, I think you are saying aloud some thoughts that many of us have had at one time or another.

- This is how you must think.
- You're wrong. This is the best way to think about what happened. . . .
- Don't be so negative.
- You're making everyone else feel bad.
- How do you expect to feel better if you take that attitude?

Can you explain a little more about the notion of a healing theory and why it is important? Is it necessary even if my child has been fairly unaffected by world events such as terrorism and war?

A family may cope well without an explicit healing theory. But why not make it explicit? Imagine an average family who is well aware of recent terrorist actions in the world but who does not discuss them very much. Even if the kids were doing fine, wouldn't it be nice to take the opportunity to discuss *why* the family or nation is coping well? Might it not be helpful to teach the children how—despite tragedy—the country is standing united and overcoming adversity? And if the children or other family members were affected in some way by the tragedy, developing an explicit healing theory may help them cope better. For example, if a parent really believes the notion that "God has a plan for my life that is good—so no matter what happens, that plan is still God's desire for me" imagine how well that parent will cope during adversity. And if that philosophy is passed on, the children may be better able to cope, too.

A healing theory does not need to be religious or spiritual. Whatever each family finds comforting and optimistic is likely to be effective. One family I know tried to cope after their teenage son died in a car accident. Initially their grief was laced with tremendous guilt. Why did they yell at him so often? Why didn't they appreciate his presence more? Over time, members would tell stories of the boy, stories that were funny and sentimental, stories that brought tears and laughter to the discussion. Over many months they began to believe they had done nothing wrong. The death was a tragedy. Their goal was to remember that life is precious and that loving others is paramount. They started a scholarship fund in his name and vowed to live their lives more conscious of how other people might be suffering and to try to ease that suffering whenever possible. They held religious beliefs and believed that the boy had many wonderful qualities and would be waiting for them in heaven. Their healing theory helped them make sense of something that seemed senseless. And it united them.

28

More Sample Conversations

No work is hard when there is love.

—Bishop Fulton J. Sheen

I thought the world would crumble
I thought the world would fall
I thought we wouldn't get through it
That we wouldn't make it at all

Then the world came together
The world stood tall
The world became united
United through it all.

—Courtney K., age 13

The young brother and sister threw the last remaining bread pieces on the ground for the ducks to eat. The morning was chilly. The pond would freeze over in the coming winter weeks.

"But they're still hungry!" the boy cried.

"Can we go home and bring back some more bread?" the girl asked her father.

"They'll be fine," their dad answered. "They know how to look for food. They'll find it somewhere." He buttoned up his son's jacket. "It's getting colder," he said. "Let's get going."

The children watched from the car window as the ducks waddled and flapped by the water's edge. They knew that their dad was probably right. The ducks would surely find more food. But yet they wondered if they had done enough for them.

Sometimes when parents tell me how they spoke to their children about some serious issue, the image of feeding the ducks comes to my mind. The parents spoke with love and concern to their kids, offering them pieces of love and wisdom. But was it enough? Were the children satisfied? If not, where will they go for more answers? For surely they will get more answers as time goes on. But will they be the best answers—answers that the parents would want their children to learn?

During troubling times when the world becomes a scary place, when loved ones die, when normal routines and dreams are suspended temporarily in order to cope with fears, grief, or the current crisis, parents need to be more available to their kids. *Comments need not always provide solutions, but comfort. Conversations need not be lengthy, just revisited.* Communicating with children is a work in progress. Children must believe that parents are always available to them, that the future is still hopeful, and that no fear or concern is so upsetting that it can't be talked about.

Sample Conversations

Keep in mind the SAFE approach:

S   **Search** for hidden, unstated concerns.

A   **Actions** that your children can take to feel influential

F   **Feel feelings**—don't dismiss a child's feelings right away.

E   **Ease minds.** Offer hope.

It is certainly possible that one of your conversations will be brief and effective and might go something like this:

"Mom, will terrorists kill us?"

"No."

"Good. Can you take me to the mall later?"

Then again, it is hard to judge just how effective that was without getting additional feedback from your child.

Sample #1

Imagine that the above conversation continues this way:

Mom: Yes, we can go to the mall. (Searching:) You seem worried about terrorists.

Child: Not too much.

M: What made you ask about it?

C: One of my friends was talking about it yesterday. She heard something on the news about a terrorist alert.

M: I see. Yes, there have been reports like that. It is a little scary. Is that how you feel (Feel feelings)?

C: I guess. Most days I don't worry too much. I just wish there were no terrorists.

M: Most people feel a little scared occasionally. I know that the government is doing a lot of work to stop terrorists. But it will take some time to do the job.

C: Yeah.

M: When I get nervous I just try to go about my business and do the things I ordinarily would do. That takes my mind off of worrying (Action step).

C: Do you think there will be more terrorism?

M: There probably will be. But I also believe there will be a lot less of it as time goes on (Ease minds).

C: What time can we go shopping?

M: How about three o'clock? I'm glad you spoke to me about terrorism. I want us to talk about it again some time.

C: Okay.

In the above scenario, the girl wasn't interested in a lengthy discussion. But at least she was reassured for the time being and discovered that her mom was willing to talk. The mother did a good job probing. She could easily have ended the discussion earlier but pushed it a little further. She also validated her daughter's feelings ("Most people feel a little scared . . ." when another parent might have told his child not to feel that way. She made her daughter feel better by offering realistic reassurances, not by telling her she was wrong to be concerned.

Sample #2

Now imagine a scenario where the worries hit closer to home. It doesn't matter what the worries are. Maybe a parent is seriously ill. Maybe a loved one is near death or has just died. Maybe there were some robberies in the neighborhood or some other frightening local event. What matters is how the parent or caretaker responds.

Child: I thought Mom would be back to work by now.

Dad: So did we. When she lost her job a few months ago we thought she would find another job soon. But that hasn't happened.

C: What happens if she doesn't get a job?

D: Good question. We need the money she earns. Already we have had to buy fewer things. We would really have to be careful not to spend money unless we absolutely had to.

C: Will we have to move?

D: No. We would try to make sure that didn't happen. Mom could always find a job somewhere and make money, but she wouldn't necessarily get a job that paid her what she was earning before. It would be tight for us. But we could get by.

C: Okay.

D: (Searching:) What do you think of what I've been saying?

C: I don't know.

D: Some kids your age would be a little worried. Other kids might not think much about it.

C: I guess I'm a little worried.

D: (Feel feelings) That's okay. What worries you the most?

C: That we might be poor.

D: (Ease minds) That won't happen. I'm still working and Mom can always get some sort of job. We will manage.

C: Will we have enough food?

D: Absolutely. It is the extras that we have to cut back on. We may not go on vacation this year. And we can't buy expensive clothes. (Action step:) Can you think of ways you can help us to save money?"

C: I won't ask for stuff.

D: That would help us. Actually, sometimes you can still ask. But you may not be able to get it.

C: All right.

Sample #3

The time when parents are least likely to talk about some tragedy or loss is long after it has happened. Presuming that their kids are adjusting adequately they may convince themselves that revisiting the topic is unnecessary or that it might bring back feelings of fear or pain. Actually, it is a good idea to get feedback from your child. And even if your child was personally unaffected by some world or national event, such as the attack on the Pentagon and the World Trade Center, those events may have influenced your child's outlook on life or the future.

Imagine this following discussion with a teenager. (By the way, even less talkative teens might be more willing to open up in certain situations such as a long car drive, eating in a restaurant, or while overhearing a news bulletin. Look for opportune moments.) The conversation does not get very far because the teen, being fairly typical, is not very forthcoming. What's important is that the parent at least set a tone for the conversation and showed an interest in dialogue.

Parent: A lot has happened in the world in recent years. Wars and terrorism especially. We were fortunate that no one in our family was killed or injured by those things. Do you ever think about terrorism or war?

Teenager: Sometimes. Not much.

P: The world isn't in the kind of shape parents wanted it to be for their children. (Search:) How has terrorism affected you? Do you think differently or feel different about life than you once did?

T: I wonder if there will be a bigger war, or if I'll have to fight in a war.

P: It's not what you planned on.

T: No.

P: Given everything that has happened in the world and in our country in the last few years, are you more impressed with humanity or less impressed?

T: That's hard to say.

P: What's your gut feeling? Do you think people are basically good and try to do what's right? Or do you think people are more selfish?

T: Can I think about it?

P: Sure.

Sample #4

Imagine that your preteen child hears about the latest terrorism attempt.

Parent: You were watching the news when they talked about the man who tried to blow up the plane.

Child: Yeah.

P: (Searching) What did you think about that?

C: I don't know.

P: I wish things like this weren't happening in the world.

C: Did they get the bad guy?

P: Yes, they did. The police are very good at capturing these terrorists.

C: Will we ever go on a plane?

P: Some day. We've been on planes before. The first time was when you were just a baby.

C: (Stays quiet)

P: (Searching) I wonder if you are worried about being on a plane?

C: A little.

P: (Feel feelings) That's normal to feel that way. I would feel a little nervous, too, if I had to get on a plane. (Ease minds:) But I still would get on one.

C: What if someone tried to blow it up?

P: If I thought that could really happen then I wouldn't get on the plane in the first place. (Ease minds:) I really think that the plane will be safe.

C: But you can't tell for sure.

P: That's right. Nobody can tell these things for sure. But I still don't think anything bad would happen to us. (Action step:) How about some day we go to the airport and watch the planes take off and land? We can have lunch there, too. We won't get on a plane, we'll just watch.

C: Okay.

P: Maybe if we do that you'll be less worried.

C: Maybe.

P: Do you know how many planes fly each day in our country? About ten thousand.

C: Really?

P: That's a lot. And that's every day. If planes were unsafe we'd be hearing about bombings and crashes practically every day. But we don't hear those stories because planes are very safe.

C: (Stays quiet)

P: Even though planes are very safe, I still don't like hearing bad things in the news. (Searching:) Are you still worried about that or are you thinking of something else?

That conversation might continue or not, depending on the child's answer to the last question. What's important is that the parent took the time to discuss the issue instead of saying something like "Don't worry about things like that" which would have been a mistake.

When I use the SAFE approach to talking with my children, I find I am most unsure about the "feel feelings" component. Specifically, when my kids express a feeling I don't want them to have—such as fear—I keep thinking that if I validate that feeling it will only persist, when what I really want is for them to NOT feel that way. How can I tell my kids that they don't need to feel a certain way without violating the "Feel feelings" rule?

Understanding a child's feelings—and communicating that those feelings make sense to you—is not the same as agreeing with those feelings. For example, if your best friend loved to ride on roller coasters and you were petrified of them, she would validate your feelings by saying something like, "A lot of people feel the way you do. But I get a thrill out of rides like that." She didn't agree that roller coasters were frightening, she simply let you know that your feelings made sense. If she were to say, "Oh, you're being silly!" you would have not felt understood and you probably would have been annoyed.

If your child is afraid of something and you want to convince him that he doesn't have to feel that way, you are better off validating his feelings first. Let him know that his feelings are not unusual. (All of us are more likely to listen to good advice when we first feel understood.) *Then* you can tell him why you disagree with his views or what he can do to feel better.

If all a child hears when he expresses a negative feeling is something like, "Don't feel that way" he will probably learn that expressing himself is a useless activity.

References

Aboud, Frances and Doyle, Anna. Does talk of race foster prejudice or tolerance in children. *Canadian Journal of Behavioural Science*, 28 (1996): 161–170.

Augoustinos, Martha and Rosewarne, Dana. Stereotype knowledge and prejudice in children. *British Journal of Developmental Psychology*, 19 (2001): 143–156.

Coleman, Paul. *How to Say It to Your Kids: The Right Words to Solve Problems, Soothe Feelings, and Teach Values*. New Jersey: Prentice-Hall, 2000.

Figley, Charles. *Helping Traumatized Families*. San Francisco: Jossey-Bass, 1989.

Groves, B., Zuckerman, B., Marons, S., and Cohen, D. Silent victims: Children who witness violence. *Journal of the American Medical Association*, 269 (1993): 262–264.

Haidt, Jonathan. Elevation and the revelation of our better selves. *Research News and Opportunities in Science and Theology*. October, 2 (2), 2001. p. 20.

Katz, Mark. *On Playing a Poor Hand Well: Insights from the Lives of those Who Have Overcome Childhood Risks and Adversities*. New York: W.W. Norton, 1997.

LaGreco, A., Silverman, W., Vernberg, E., and Prinstein, M. Symptoms of stress in children after Hurricane Andrew: A prospective study. *Journal of Consulting and Clinical Psychology*, 64 (1996): 712–723.

Masten, Ann and Coatsworth, Douglas J. The development of competence in favorable and unfavorable environments. *American Psychologist*, 53 (1998): 205–220.

Park, Lee. Families cope with explaining war. *The Poughkeepsie Journal*, October 8, 2001, p. 1D

Porterfiedl, Kay Marie. *Straight Talk about Post Traumatic Stress Disorder*. New York: Facts on File, Inc., 1996.

Quadagno, D., Eberstein, I., Foster, K., Sittig, J., Sly, D., and Kistner, J. Magic Johnson and children's concepts of AIDS. *AIDS Education and Prevention*, 9 (1997): 359–372.

Sheen, Fulton. *Simple Truths: Thinking Through Life with Fulton J. Sheen*. Missouri: Liguori/Triumph, 1998, p. 74.

Staudacher, Carol. *A Time to Grieve: Meditations for Healing After the Death of a Loved One*. San Francisco: Harper San Francisco, 1994.

Index

PAR
155.4136
C

Coleman, Paul W.

How to say it to your
child when bad
things happen.

$14.00

33910009082349
08/01/2003

DATE			

GLOBETROTTER™

Travel Guide

GREEK
ISLANDS

PAUL HARCOURT DAVIES

NEW
HOLLAND

NEW
HOLLAND

★★★ Highly recommended
★★ Recommended
★ See if you can

Fifth edition published in 2008
by New Holland Publishers (UK) Ltd
London • Cape Town • Sydney • Auckland
10 9 8 7 6 5 4 3 2 1
website: www.newhollandpublishers.com

Garfield House, 86 Edgware Road
London W2 2EA, United Kingdom

80 McKenzie Street
Cape Town 8001, South Africa

Unit 1, 66 Gibbes Street
Chatswood, NSW 2067, Australia

218 Lake Road, Northcote,
Auckland, New Zealand

Distributed in the USA by
The Globe Pequot Press, Connecticut

ISBN 978 1 84773 193 7

Publishing Manager: Thea Grobbelaar
DTP Cartographic Manager: Genené Hart
Editors: Thea Grobbelaar, Alicha van Reenen,
Melany McCallum
Cartographers: Lorissa Bouwer, Tanja Spinola,
Nicole Bannister
Design and DTP: Nicole Bannister, Sonya Cupido
Picture Researchers: Emily Hedges, Sonya Meyer
Compiler/Verifier: Genené Hart
Updated by: Robin Gauldie
Reproduction by Resolution (Cape Town) and Hirt & Carter
(Pty) Ltd, Cape Town. Printed and bound by Times Offset
(M) Sdn. Bhd., Malaysia.

Photographic Credits:
John Frick, pages 18, 56, 90; **Paul Harcourt Davies**,
pages 8, 9, 10, 11; **LF/Dr R. Cannon**, page 53; **LF/ Jeremy
Hoare**, pages 45; **LF/Barry Mayes**, page 54; **Andreas
Nicola**, pages 27, 28; **IPB/Jeanetta Baker**, page 70;
IPB/Peter Baker, pages 21, 22, 71, 108, 110, 118, 93, 94,
100, 103; **IPB/Gary Goodwin**, pages 17, 33, 34, 74;
Picture Bank Photo Library (PBPL), pages 7, 14, 24, 44
(top), 77, 78, 79; **Pictures Colour Library**, cover; **RHPL**,
title page, pages 4, 20, 59, 66, 68, 69, 82, 92 (top and
bottom), 89, 96, 104, 102, 111 ; **RHPL/ David Beatty**,
pages 26, 86; **RHPL/F. Dubes**, page 83; **RHPL/Robert
Francis**, page 55; **RHPL/Lee Frost**, page 40; **RHPL/Tony
Gervis**, page 30; **RHPL/Michael Jenner**, pages 15;
RHPL/G. Kavallierakis, pages 36, 42, 48, 61; **RHPL/J.
Lightfoot**, page 50; **RHPL/Rolf Richardson**, page 88;
RHPL/Michael Short, page 115; **RHPL/E. Simanor**, page
81; **RHPL/Susan Griggs Agency**, page 57; **RHPL/G. White**,
page 19; **RHPL/Rob Whitrow**, pages 52, 112, 116;
RHPL/Adam Woolfitt, page 12; **Peter Ryan**, pages 16, 25,
29; **Spectrum Colour Library**, page 95; **ZEFA**, page 97.
[LF = Life File; IPB = International PhotoBank; RHPL =
Robert Harding Picture Library]

Keep us Current:
Information in travel guides is apt to change, which is why
we regularly update our guides. We'd be grateful to receive
feedback if you've noted something we should include in
our updates. If you have new information, please share it
with us by writing to the Publishing Manager, Globetrotter,
at the office nearest to you (addresses on this page). The
most significant contribution to each new edition will
receive a free copy of the updated guide.

Note:
In the transliteration of place names from Greek to
English spellings, various authors have tried to convey
Greek sounds in different ways. The Greek gamma is not
a simple 'g' but is more gutteral or can have a 'y' sound.
thus many different spellings are encountered. For example, Agios meaning 'saint', and used in all church names
(e.g. Agios Yioryiou) can also be spelt Aghios or Ayios.
Similarly 'dh' is sometimes used to convey the soft 'th'
sound of a Greek delta – elsewhere you might find a
simple 'd'. To avoid confusion, all accents have been
omitted from the place names in this guide.

This guidebook has been written by independent authors
and updaters. The information therein represents their
impartial opinion, and neither they nor the publishers
accept payment in return for including in the book or
writing more favourable reviews of any of the establish-
ments. Whilst every effort has been made to ensure that
this guidebook is as accurate and up to date as possible,
please be aware that the facts quoted are subject to
change, particularly the price of food, transport and
accommodation. The Publisher accepts no responsibility
or liability for any loss, injury or inconvenience incurred
by readers or travellers using this guide.

Cover: *Beautiful blue and white, Santorini island.*
Title Page: *Yachts in line at the quay in Symi harbour.*